T0273981

HIDDEN HISTORY
of
NEWARK, NEW JERSEY

Helen Lippman

THE
History
PRESS

Published by The History Press
Charleston, SC
www.historypress.com

Front cover: courtesy of the Essex County Department of Parks, Recreation, and Cultural Affairs.
Back cover: Library of Congress, LC-DIG-ggbain-12622.

First published 2024

Manufactured in the United States

ISBN 9781467152617

Library of Congress Control Number: 2023947096

CONTENTS

Acknowledgements   5
Introduction   7

I. COLONIAL DAYS
1. The Price of a City   11
2. A Storm Sparks a Schism   17
3. When Washington Came to Newark   24

II. LEADER IN INDUSTRY
4. City of Gold   31
5. Centuries of Cider   37
6. Newark's Sherlock Takes on Radium   43

III. NOTABLE FIRSTS
7. Patent Leather and Beyond   51
8. Birth of the Beer Can   56
9. Introducing the County Park   62

IV. IDEOLOGY AND ACTIVISM
10. Going Underground   71
11. Fighting for Women's Suffrage   78
12. Chasing Communists   85
13. Newark to Nazis: Get Out   90
14. Women in the Cockpit   94

V. RELIGION AND CULTURE
15. A Cleric's Dream, a Century in the Making   103
16. Tibetan Art at the Altar   109
17. Just Jazz   114

VI. NEWARK NOW
18. Urban Farming Grows Up   121
19. From Injustice to Healing   126
20. Mural City   131
21. A Place to Call Home   137

Bibliography   141
About the Author   144

Acknowledgements

As I conducted research for this book, I found help and encouragement at every turn. I'm grateful for the assistance I received from William Peniston and Andrea Ko at the Newark Museum of Art; James Amemasor at the New Jersey Historical Society; and Teresa Vega, a genealogist and historian who writes about the house on Warren Street, built by her ancestors, that served as a stop on the Underground Railroad. Many thanks, too, to Craig Mainor of Newark's United Community Corporation for taking the time to tell me the story—and success—of Hope Village; and to Julia Lauria-Blum, curator of the permanent exhibit at the American Airpower Museum that recognizes and honors the Women Airforce Service Pilots for their work during World War II. A heartfelt thanks as well to Marc Oshima, chief marketing officer at AeroFarms, and Charles Rosen, CEO of Ironbound Farm and Ciderhouse, for taking the time to tell me about their agricultural enterprises.

Many thanks especially to the late Josie Zeman, a close friend and writing-editing consultant who graciously read and commented on an earlier draft of this book; and to my loving and supportive family: daughters Jen and Diane Collins, sons-in-law Ian Bellayr and Jordan Hollender and grandson Joshua Hollender.

INTRODUCTION

I'm a proud third-generation Newarker. I was born and raised in the city and lived there for the first twenty-plus years of my life, returning to attend college, take in the culture, do volunteer work and engage in community activism. After retiring from a career in medical and healthcare publishing, I began writing about the burgeoning revitalization of my hometown. My memoir-in-essays, *To Newark with Love: A City, a Family, a Life*, was published by Fonthill Media/America Through Time in the spring of 2023, just as I was nearing completion of this book.

Although I've been involved in Newark throughout my life, doing research for *Hidden History of Newark, New Jersey* led to the discovery of many fascinating things. Here are a few examples: Thomas Paine, the famed eighteenth-century activist and pamphleteer, is thought to have penned the famous first words of *The American Crisis*—"These are the times that try men's souls"—while camped out in Military Park with the Continental army. Not only has Newark rapidly become a mural city with an interactive public art map, but it also boasts what is believed to be the longest mural in the country at one and one-third miles. And, most surprising to me, Newark was the nation's jewelry capital, not for a short time but for the better part of a century. My hope is that as you read the essays in this book, you'll find numerous aspects of Newark throughout the centuries that will both surprise and delight you.

PART I

COLONIAL DAYS

1

THE PRICE OF A CITY

Newark's founding is a complex story, involving everyone from the British monarchy and a group of dissident Puritans to the governor of colonial New Jersey and the Native Americans who laid claim to the land. Among the varying viewpoints and versions, one aspect of the settlement is abundantly clear: the price the founders paid for it. Besides appearing in documents dating from 1666, the details of the transaction are cast in stone. Literally.

Monument to the First Settlers of Newark, a statue of a Puritan atop a mausoleum standing some twenty-two feet high, commemorates Newark's founding. Besides a list of every item included in the land swap, the monument bears the names or marks of both the Puritans and the Indians who signed off on it. It also has an image of vessels like the ones from which the Puritans disembarked on the western banks of the Passaic River and a reproduction of the original layout of the settlement, apportioned into six-acre lots.

Typically referred to simply as Settlers' Monument, it occupies pride of place at Fairmount Cemetery in the city's West Ward. The 150-acre cemetery was founded in 1854. The monument was dedicated thirty years later, after the remains of settlers who had been interred in the Old Burying Ground on Broad Street and Branford Place were exhumed and reburied in a crypt at its base.

Before delving into the details of the land swap, let's take a closer look at how and why Newark was settled, as well as the man known as its founding father. Robert Treat, whose name has long been emblazoned on a hotel in

THE LANDING AT NEWARK, MAY 1666.

A scene on Settlers' Monument shows the Puritans sailing along the Passaic River. *Helen Lippman.*

downtown Newark and is well known to city residents to this day, was born in the village of Pitminster in Somerset, England, in 1624. He and his family left their home in the early 1630s. They joined waves of Puritans who set sail for the New World, seeking the freedom to live out their religious beliefs without persecution.

While the religious life they sought was considerably more stringent than that espoused by the British monarchy at the time, they did not sever ties with the Church of England. The Puritans remained Congregationalists while forging a theocracy in their new home.

Thus, no separation of church and state existed in the New Haven (Connecticut) community where Treat's family eventually settled. The colony comprised a trio of settlements known as Branford, Guilford and Milford. Founded in 1638, the New Haven colony permitted only church members to own or inherit land, have their children baptized, hold office and participate fully in the life of the community. The colony flourished in this manner, but only for a time.

In the next decade, monumental changes took place in the motherland. Civil war erupted in England in the 1640s, the result of deep religious differences and disputes about the power, policies and purse of the monarchy.

In 1648, King Charles I, Britain's reigning monarch, was found guilty of treason. He was beheaded, and the monarchy was abolished the following year. Oliver Cromwell and the Parliamentarians ultimately prevailed.

Cromwell looked far more favorably on the Puritans than the monarchy had, prompting many of those who had fled the country to head back. John Davenport, the Puritan minister who founded the New Haven colony, briefly considered joining them but ultimately opted to remain in the New World.

Then, in another ten years or so, British rule underwent another abrupt about-face. In 1658, Cromwell died and was posthumously convicted of treason. Soon after, the monarchy was restored, and Charles II, son of the beheaded king, took the throne. The agreement that would govern his reign, however, required concessions to religious tolerance.

The Royal Charter of 1662, signed by Charles II, was a crucial outcome of the new policy. The charter permitted the Connecticut settlers to make many of their own rules—in effect, to govern themselves. Without the approval of the New Haven Puritans or even their leaders being notified, the colony was absorbed into the larger Connecticut settlement, which included colonies that were far less stringent religiously. Thus the merger was a death knell for the Puritan theocracy.

Many members of the New Haven colony accepted the more liberal standards. But a group of dissidents, Robert Treat foremost among them, staunchly objected. Unlike the merged community they found themselves a part of, they insisted that only members of the Puritan church be allowed to vote, have their children baptized and participate fully in the life of the colony. Before long, they were ready to move on.

In 1666, Treat, accompanied by a man named John Gregory, headed south in search of a new home. They met with Philip Carteret, the new royal governor of New Jersey. Carteret had only recently assumed the position, after the British seized control of the land that had been governed by the Dutch and known as New Netherland.

In scouting out potential settlement sites with Carteret, Treat and his companion rejected a swath of land in South Jersey in an area that would later become Burlington. Instead, they opted for an area not far from Carteret's settlement in Elizabethtown, up what would later be named Newark Bay and on the western banks of the Passaic River.

It's not hard to understand why. The land was ripe for development, its forests filled with oak, chestnut, hickory, elm and maple trees; its land primed for farming; the river and bay teeming with fish and seafood; and the grounds home to an abundance of deer, elk, beaver, otter, wolves and foxes.

The area also had an ample supply of salt marshes for grazing. What's more, Treat was given to understand that the original agreement entered into with the Lenni Lenape Indians cleared the way for the new settlement.

So it was that in May 1666—historians cite the date as May 17 or 18—Treat and a band of some thirty Puritans sailed down the Passaic River and arrived at their new home. Elizabeth Swaine, a young woman of nineteen, is believed to have been the first person to step ashore, aided by the man whom she would later marry.

Scarcely had the settlers begun unloading their belongings, however, when a group of Native Americans confronted them. This land is our land, was the message the Indians conveyed as they ordered the Puritans to depart and leave it unscathed.

Dismayed, the settlers loaded some of their belongings back on the boats and sought counsel from Carteret. The problem, it appeared, was that Treat—unbeknown to him—had been expected to present a letter from the governor to the Indian chief. Because this wasn't done, the impasse remained to be addressed.

In an attempt to properly secure the land for their fledgling settlement, Treat and a handful of others headed north to negotiate with the Hackensack Indians, as the local tribe of the Lenni Lenape was known. Samuel Edsai, a New Jersey landowner who was fluent in Unami, the language spoken by the Natives in the area, accompanied them. Together, they hammered out a deal.

In exchange for a range of goods valued at $750, the New Haven Puritans secured a large swath of land, from a mountain range to the west all the way to the bay. A list of the items the Indians received—ranging from axes to booze to wampum—prompted one local historian to conclude that "the Indians sold the Puritans all the land from the crest of the Watchung Mountains to the Newark Basin for trinkets."

That, however, is a slight overstatement. The things the Lenni Lenape received, collectively valued at $750, were a bit more substantial than trinkets. The inscription on Settlers' Monument describes the deal in the following way:

> These lands were sold in consideration of "fifty double hands of powder, one hundred bars of lead, twenty axes, twenty coates, ten guns, twenty pistolls, ten swords, four blankets, four barrells of beer, ten pairs of breeches, fifty knives, twenty howes, eight hundred and fifty fathoms of wampum, twenty ankors of licquers or something equivalent and three trooper's coates; and to the top of the mountain for two guns, three coates and thirteen horns of rum."

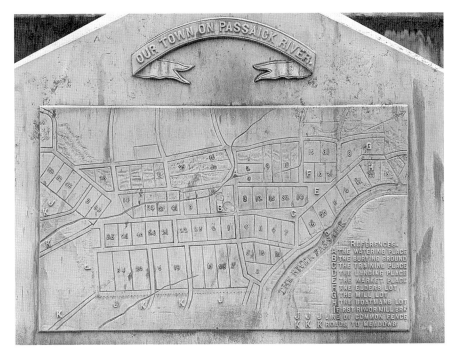

A map of "Our Town on Passaick River," as laid out by founder Robert Treat in 1666. *Helen Lippman.*

(A fathom of wampum was about six feet long and contained some 240 to 360 beads, and the deal that signed away the land all the way to the top of the mountain was negotiated at a later date.)

And so the fledgling settlement was born. A theocracy like the New Haven colony the Puritans came from, the new community defrayed the cost of the land by dividing the $750 payout among all new residents in the settlement's first year of existence. Treat plotted the settlement in a grid, sliced into the plots as shown on the monument, with an early map referring to the land on the banks of the Passaic. In exchange for his leadership, Treat received a double plot on the Four Corners, as Newark's earliest and largest thoroughfare was known. It later became the intersection of Broad and Market Streets—one of the most heavily trafficked locations in the nation.

The settlement was not called Newark right away. Initially identified as Milford for the New Haven settlement Treat hailed from, its name was changed when Abraham Pierson, the community's first pastoral leader, arrived. Pierson, born in Newark-on-Trent in England, wanted to call the settlement New-Ark, for his hometown and, some say, as a reference to the New Ark of the Covenant. Some historians posit that the intended name was New-Work.

Over time, pronunciation shifted, and the settlement—and later the city—became known as Newark (*New*-ark), with the emphasis on the first syllable. In recent years, yet another iteration has emerged: many residents of New Jersey's largest city have adopted the monosyllabic *Nork*.

2

A STORM SPARKS A SCHISM

Newark was the Puritans' final New World settlement—their last chance to establish the "theocracy of Zion" so many had struggled for years to create. For decades after the settlement's founding in 1666, church and state were indivisible.

Old First, which has been called "the church that founded Newark," was the settlement's first public building. Erected on the west side of Broad Street—believed to be the widest street in colonial America—it was a modest structure consisting of little more than a single room. Meeting minutes from September 10, 1668, indicate that a committee oversaw the construction of the church, in which virtually all able-bodied men participated. Civic and military affairs were conducted here, as were religious services. After the structure's completion, residents were summoned to prayer by the beating of a drum.

The church had an additional purpose: It served as a place to guard against attacks by Native Americans and to offer refuge to colonists in the event of such an occurrence. Thus, in 1675, the settlers built protective "appendages"—some called them flankers—at the corners of the building. Theoretically, at least, soldiers could use them as hiding places from which to take command from every direction.

Old First began life in 1644 in Branford, one of a trio of villages making up the New Haven (Connecticut) colony. The church relocated to Newark about a year after the Puritans did, when Reverend Abraham Pierson moved to the new settlement to continue as its spiritual leader.

First Presbyterian Church, known as Old First, was organized soon after the settlers arrived. *Helen Lippman.*

In Newark's earliest years, only church members were permitted to own land, vote, hold office, have their children baptized and participate fully in community affairs. Officially, the Fundamental Agreements—the rules by which the theocracy was to be governed—remained in place until well into the eighteenth century. In reality, this staunchly Puritanical foundation began to show cracks in little more than a decade after Newark's 1666 founding.

As newcomers to both the New World and Newark flocked to the settlement because of its ideal locale and abundance of farmland, fish, game and timber, this "iron bedstead" rule rapidly became unsustainable. Records of a town meeting in 1677 indicate that "all and every man that improves land in the town of Newark" were expected to show up at meetings and "attend to any business that shall be proposed." Church membership, this suggests, had ceased to be a prerequisite for voting or land-ownership.

Yet whatever unofficial shift in practice had begun to occur was never formalized. Nor did it have widespread acceptance. About eight years after those minutes were drafted, community leaders appointed a committee tasked with going house to house to interrogate anyone who was not in compliance with the theocracy's covenant. Indeed, the church's supervision over personal and public life was so strict, stated a note in a WPA New Jersey guide, that "early Newark was more puritan than much of New England itself."

In the decades that followed, the death of Newark's founding members and a steady stream of settlers from abroad further eroded the church's most stringent tenets. Presbyterianism began thriving in the New World as well. So it happened that in 1720, driven largely by immigrants and settlers favoring a less rigid religious community, Old First transitioned from a Congregationalist to a Presbyterian church. While there is little doubt that the demise of one-church governance in Newark was inevitable, the singular event that put the proverbial final nail in its coffin can be traced to an act not of man but of God. It occurred in the fall of 1733, in the form of a torrential rainstorm.

In fact, it was not a solitary storm but days of heavy precipitation—enough to destroy much of the as-yet-unharvested wheat grown by one Colonel Josiah Ogden. The colonel was the son of Elizabeth Swaine, said to be the first Puritan settler to step onto the western bank of the Passaic River in 1666.

Ogden was a pillar of the community, portrayed as a man of "energy, wealth, and influence." He was a devout church member as well. Yet he committed the sin of Sabbath-breaking. His sin, it turned out, was to harvest his crops on a Sunday.

Ogden, historical documents indicate, subscribed to the belief that "the Sabbath was made for man, not man for the Sabbath." The point, as detailed in Scriptures, was that the weekly day of rest was a blessing, rather than a burden, for believers.

In retrospect, it seemed obvious that Ogden had acted neither carelessly nor irrationally. The simple truth, it appeared, was that the colonel decided to harvest his wheat on that ill-fated Sunday sixty-seven years after Newark's founding because he knew that to do otherwise would have resulted in its total ruin. That did not stop church leaders from publicly sanctioning him for defying one of its key tenets. This so infuriated the colonel that he withdrew from Old First, vowing to find another church—even if it meant building one himself.

The leaders of Old First Presbyterian, as the church was then known, ultimately revoked the sanctions, realizing in retrospect that extenuating circumstances likely justified Ogden's action. But for the colonel, the change of heart came too late. He took his complaint to the Presbyterian Synod of Philadelphia, where the denomination had begun holding meetings of its regional governing body in 1717. Presbyterianism had spread rapidly throughout the colonies, with congregations led primarily by pastors from Ireland and Scotland.

At the same time, the Church of England had sent a group of missionaries, known as the Society for the Propagation of the Gospel in Foreign Parts, to nearby Elizabethtown. By 1729, if not earlier, Episcopalian services had become a regular occurrence in the greater Newark area. Two or three years later, an Episcopalian emissary wrote to friends in England to report that he had been preaching to an ever-increasing number of people "at Newark, Whippany and in the mountains."

Eager for a more satisfactory church in which to worship, Ogden wasted no time in making contact with local Episcopalian preachers. He busied himself, too, rallying Newarkers who were growing increasingly dissatisfied with both Presbyterian dogma and the colony's single-church governance. His timing could hardly have been better. Although the majority of Newarkers remained committed to Old First, it was not hard to find residents who had begun using the Church of England's (Episcopalian) Book of Common Prayer. That is, there was an adequate number of people in Ogden's camp to result in a bitter schism. Alexander MacWhorter, minister of Old First from 1759 to 1807, later lamented the rift. "This separation," he declared, "was the origin of the greatest animosity and alienation between friends and townsmen, Christians, neighbors, and relatives that this town ever beheld."

In 1743, Trinity Church, described by the late Newark historian Charles Cummings as "the second steeple to pierce the colonial sky over Newark," was erected. Situated on Broad Street not far from Old First, Trinity was sixty-three by forty-five feet and had a twenty-seven-foot ceiling and a ninety-five-foot steeple. Three years later, England's King George II granted a charter for the new church, and Trinity's first pastor, the Reverend Isaac Browne, arrived. Dated 1746, the charter of record is a sheepskin document, restored and preserved by the New Jersey Historical Society.

During the Revolutionary War, both Trinity and Old First served as field hospitals for British and Patriot troops. While each treated soldiers regardless of which side they fought on, the two churches remained on opposite sides of the conflict.

Trinity's Isaac Browne was a British Loyalist, forced to flee when victory for the Patriots was imminent. MacWhorter, who served First Presbyterian

Part of the tower of Trinity Church, Newark's second-oldest house of worship, dates from 1743. *Library of Congress.*

throughout the war, remained faithful to George Washington. The rancor between Newark's Protestants and Episcopalians did not cease, he later recalled, until the conclusion of the war. In the years since, both congregations have undergone a number of iterations.

Characterized by a historian as "anything but imposing," the first Old First was "four or six and twenty foot wide, and thirty foot long and ten foot between joints." Its replacement—that is, the second Old First—was a bit larger, at approximately forty-four feet in both width and length. Exactly when it was erected remains uncertain. Construction likely began sometime between April 1714 and August 1716, a period for which there exists "a vacancy" in the records.

What is clear is that the second Old First stood on the west side of Broad Street a little to the north of the earlier edifice. Damage incurred as a result of the church's use as a field hospital during the war led to construction of Old First's third—and final—building shortly after the end of the Revolutionary War.

Known as First Presbyterian Church and Cemetery, the "new" Old First was built in 1787, this time on the east side of Broad Street. It has been in continuous use since then and was added to the National Register of Historic Places in 1972.

In the late 1880s, the remains of early settlers interred in the Old Burying Ground adjacent to the old First Church were transferred to a tomb at Fairmount Cemetery. The 150-acre cemetery, located in Newark's West Ward, opened in 1855, soon after burials in the heart of the city were prohibited. The action was precipitated by the fear that dead bodies contributed to the spread of yellow fever. The old burial grounds have long since been covered over, most recently by the Prudential Center and a parking deck.

Not long after the re-interment, a tribute to the early settlers of Newark was installed at Fairmount Cemetery. Dedicated on December 19, 1889, the statue—now known simply as Settlers' Monument—is cared for by the city as well as by the Newark Preservation and Landmark Committee. On its base, the sculptor detailed the terms of the transfer of the land from the Lenni Lenape Indians to the Puritan settlers; the division of plots of land; the vessels on which the first group of Puritans arrived; and more.

Like Old First, Trinity Episcopal Church incurred damage during the Revolutionary War, but the house of worship was repaired rather than rebuilt. Then, in 1804, a fire destroyed it. A few years later, it was rebuilt on almost the exact same site. The cornerstone for the new Trinity Episcopal was laid in 1809. At its completion the following year, Trinity's white steeple soared 168 feet in the air.

The church, still in use today, has undergone a variety of changes, both structural and otherwise. In 1857, a chancel and sanctuary were added on its east end. Close to a century later, in 1944, Trinity "was elevated to full cathedral status."

Twenty years after that, St. Philip's Church—a predominantly Black congregation situated on High and West Market Streets—burned down. Two years later, St. Philip's and Trinity—a predominantly white congregation—joined together. The merger, long known as Trinity & St. Philip's Cathedral and still occupying a building completed in 1810, brings together "two strong traditions of Anglican and African," the church notes on its website.

3

WHEN WASHINGTON CAME TO NEWARK

New Jersey's schoolchildren—like virtually everyone who has lived or attended school in the Garden State—know the story of General George Washington's historic Christmas Day crossing of the Delaware River. They're equally likely to be familiar with the travails of his army's encampment at Valley Forge, Pennsylvania, as well as the months that he and his troops spent huddled at their headquarters in Morristown. What they're far less likely to be aware of is that George Washington spent time in Newark as well, on one occasion rousing his troops and rapidly departing because the British were in hot pursuit. Or that Washington stayed overnight here on multiple occasions.

Charles Cummings, the late Newark historian and prolific writer, highlighted Washington's time in Newark in a *Star-Ledger* column dated May 16, 1996. The title—*Yes, George Washington Slept Here. Often, in Fact*—reflects the fact that his overnight visits to Newark were neither infrequent nor widely known. In fact, Washington was but one of many prominent Americans who made their way to Newark. But it is safe to say that none was as famous or held in as high regard as the man who led the Patriots to victory, went on to become the new nation's first president and will forever be known as the father of our country.

Washington's first known stopover in Newark was in June 1775, just two months after the start of the Revolutionary War. En route to Cambridge, Massachusetts, Washington stayed at the Eagle Tavern on Broad and Williams Streets. As he and his entourage departed, they traveled north along Broad Street, then headed east on Market Street and on to Ferry Street to cross the Passaic River. From there it was into Hoboken, where Washington and his troops crossed the Hudson River. The somewhat circuitous route was chosen, it is believed, because the river crossing was a bit out of the way, giving the troops a greater likelihood of evading capture.

When Washington next visited Newark, seventeen months had passed. By then, he and his troops were downtrodden. The Continental army was in retreat. The men who accompanied Washington were hungry, exhausted and ragged. Their uniforms—boots and all—were torn and tattered.

On the way to Newark in November 1776, Washington and his Continental army crossed the Passaic River into Aquackanonck, as Passaic was then known. The bridge they traversed was a narrow wooden structure. After making it safely to the other side and realizing that General Charles Cornwallis and his well-equipped British troops were close on their heels, the men hastily dismantled the bridge. Doing so turned out to be their saving grace.

Then the troops split up. Two contingents headed west to what is now Montclair and Glen Ridge. A third, comprising approximately 3,500 men, accompanied Washington. They marched along the river and passed through parts of what would later become Clifton, Nutley and Belleville before entering Newark. The troops arrived on the evening of November 22, 1776.

Precisely where Washington slept at this time has been a subject of considerable speculation. Some maintained that he stayed at a prominent hall on Mt. Pleasant Avenue. Others were skeptical, questioning the logic and even the safety of housing the general in what was then an out-of-the-way place. Another group was certain that he had spent the night at the stone Coe House on High Street, until closer examination revealed that this elegant building, sometimes referred to as the Glencoe Mansion, did not exist at the time. The date of record for the mansion, where Corey Booker, former Newark mayor and current U.S. senator (D-NJ), once rented a room, is 1871.

So where did Washington stay in 1776? It appears that then, as on his previous visit, he slept at the Eagle Tavern. Reports from old Newarkers who recalled hearing the tavern spoken of as "Washington's headquarters" bolstered the likelihood that this is the case. While the locale of Washington's Newark stopover was long questioned, the place where his troops camped out was never in doubt. The general's men remained day and night at Military Park, the triangular, six-acre plot of land along Broad Street. Known at the time as the Training Place—and laid out by Newark founder Robert Treat precisely for military training purposes—the grounds were visible on maps dating back to 1667.

As it happens, Thomas Paine, the acclaimed pamphleteer and advocate of revolutionary causes, was traveling with the Continental army. He, like the troops he accompanied, camped out in Newark in November. It was during this time that Paine is believed to have penned the famous opening lines of *The American Crisis*. "These are the times that try men's souls," Paine wrote. "The summer soldier and the sunshine patriot will, in this crisis, shrink from the service of their country; but he that stands by it now, deserves the love and thanks of man and woman."

After five days, the time had come to depart. The only reason Washington had been able to remain in Newark for as long as he did was because Cornwallis and his army had been delayed by having to build a new bridge. But by then, realizing the British were rapidly approaching and hamstrung by the recent capture of Washington's second-in-command, Charles Lee, the general rallied his troops and marched southwest toward the Delaware River.

While the Continental army won a victory there at Christmastime, it turned out they left Newark in the nick of time. "No sooner had Washington retreated," historian Cummings wrote, "than British forces occupied old Newark-town."

Washington returned to Newark during the winter of 1779–80, while he was headquartered at Morristown. The war raged on, of course. And while it has been reported that the general came to town both to attend meetings and to socialize, he characterized these visits as fact-finding missions.

Washington was not the only future president to come to Newark. In another *Star-Ledger* column, Cummings counted as many as eighteen current, former or future presidents who stayed here. Yet Washington was almost certainly the most venerated. When Washington died in December 1799, Essex County executives passed a resolution that called for Newarkers to honor his memory by donning black crepe armbands, tolling bells and holding funeral orations at churches and Masonic lodges. The following year, city officials proclaimed February 22, the date of Washington's birth, to be a citywide day of mourning. Although the day was observed in many municipalities for years to come, Washington's birthday did not become a federal holiday until 1879.

Some ninety years later, the celebrations of the birthdays of Washington and Abraham Lincoln merged into a single holiday known as Presidents' Day. The law that enacted that and other changes in holidays is called the Uniform Monday Holiday Act. It passed Congress in 1968 and took effect in January 1971.

Newark's reverence for Washington, however, was evident long before the twentieth century—notably, while he was still alive. In 1795, residents voted to turn the land west of Broad Street, previously used as a grazing spot for sheep and a place for Newarkers to market their goods, into Washington Park. Well over a century later, in 1912, an equestrian statue of Washington was installed there. The bronze portrait shows the general, having just dismounted from and standing next to his horse, bidding the troops a final farewell. The statue, about eight feet, six inches tall and twelve feet, six inches wide, was installed on a low, rectangular base resting atop a foliage-covered mound.

A statue of Christopher Columbus was placed in the park five years later. In June 2020, more than one hundred years after its 1917 dedication, the statue of Columbus was taken down.

While George Washington's statue remains, the park no longer bears his name. On Juneteenth (June 19), 2022, Newark mayor Ras Baraka renamed it Harriet Tubman Square. A monument depicting the noted abolitionist

This equestrian statue of George Washington bidding farewell to his troops was dedicated in 1912. *Wikipedia.*

and detailing much of her work was designed to replace the Columbus statue while incorporating the original base. The new Tubman monument, so multifaceted and full of information that it brings to mind a miniature museum, was unveiled in March 2023.

PART II

LEADER IN INDUSTRY

4

CITY OF GOLD

In January 1917, an amusing anecdote was published in the *Newark Evening News*. The article told the story of a well-to-do couple from Newark who, while vacationing in Italy, found themselves peering into the window of a jewelry store on Venice's St. Mark's Square. Pointing to an elegant platinum and ruby ring, the wife implored her husband to buy it for her. Besides being enchanted by its beauty, she told him, she wanted the ring as a reminder of the romantic Venetian nights they had enjoyed and the pleasure of being ferried about on moonlit evenings by the city's iconic gondoliers.

After carefully perusing the ring, the story goes, the husband agreed to buy it. But because he was in the jewelry business back home in New Jersey, he knew the truth: The ring his wife coveted had not been made in Venice or anywhere else in Italy or on the European continent. In fact, it had been made in Newark! Apparently, he kept that knowledge to himself, leaving his wife to forever gaze lovingly at her dazzling "Venetian" jewelry.

That anecdote features prominently in an essay by Ulysses Grant Dietz in *The Glitter & the Gold: Fashioning America's Jewelry*. The story gets top billing, wrote Dietz—who for decades served as curator of decorative arts at the Newark Museum—not simply as an amusing side note but because it highlights the city's longtime position in the national as well as international jewelry industry.

And what was that position? As then museum director Mary Sue Sweeney Price wrote in a foreword to *The Glitter & the Gold*, "In 1909, when the Museum was founded, the City of Newark was to jewelry-making what Detroit would soon become to automobile manufacturing." Newark was the country's fine-jewelry-making capital, Sweeney Price noted, "once known to the jewelry world as 'the city of gold and platinum and precious stones.'"

What's more, Newark's reign was not short-lived; it maintained that position not just for a decade or a generation or even half a century, but for close to one hundred years. As the story of the platinum ring highlights, however, Newark's preeminence in the jewelry industry was not widely known at the time. Nor is it widely known today.

A brooch of a woman in the shape of a butterfly is but one example of the fine jewelry manufactured in Newark. *The Newark Museum of Art.*

With that in mind, Dietz—one of several coauthors of *The Glitter & the Gold*—asked, and immediately answered, two important questions in an early entry in the book:

> Q: *"What did Newark jewelry shops make?"*
> A: *"The simple answer is—everything, from gold collar buttons to diamond and platinum brooches."*
>
> Q: *"Where did this Newark-made jewelry sell?"*
> A: *"Again, the answer is simple—everywhere, from Fifth Avenue to Fargo* [ND], *in every jewelry store, large and small, all across America, and in Europe as well."*

Although records show that a silversmith opened a shop in Newark in the late eighteenth century, the year 1801 officially marks the start of the city's jewelry industry. That's when Connecticut-born Epaphras Hinsdale opened Newark's first jewelry production shop. Hinsdale's shop was the first of its kind in both the state and the nation. What is most significant, however, is that Hinsdale aimed not simply to make and sell jewelry but also to manufacture it in large enough quantities to be marketed far afield. That intent marked a major shift in perspective. *The Glitter & the Gold* describes the concept as "a remarkable breakthrough." Prior to that time, American-made jewelry was not mass-produced but made to order.

In the years that followed, Hinsdale partnered with a man by the name of John Taylor. Taylor subsequently teamed up with Colonel Isaac Baldwin, reportedly "the first in the nation to undertake quality manufacture of American-made jewelry." Indeed, some seventy years after the launch of Hinsdale's enterprise, the annual output of Newark's ever-growing number of jewelry manufacturing firms totaled $5 million, an amount equaled only by that of the city's long-established leather-making industry. Further testimony to the city's jewelry-making prowess came in 1878, in the landmark book *The History of Newark, New Jersey: Narrative of Its Rise and Progress*. By then, the city was turning out items "rivaling the beauty, finish and design not only of the richest handiwork of Europe, but the rare and exquisite jewelry…of the Egyptians, Assyrians, Babylonians, Etruscans and Romans," author Joseph Atkinson declared.

By 1929, shortly before the stock market crash, the number of jewelry manufacturing firms in Newark had swelled to 144; they collectively produced jewelry worth more than $22 million per year. By then, Dietz wrote, the city was one of the world's largest purchasers of gemstones, and "it was said that ninety percent of all solid-gold jewelry made in the United States came from Newark factories." Yet as the story of the ring sold in Venice so clearly shows, hardly anyone knew it outside of those in the industry.

The fact that Newark specialized in the manufacture rather than the retail sale of fine jewelry is largely what kept it out of the public eye. Until the 1890s, when Newark manufacturers began adding what Dietz delicately described as "little touch marks" as code for wholesale buyers, city-made creations were sold totally unmarked. The names of internationally renowned jewelers like Tiffany and Cartier were often added later. Yet this was not fraud, *New York Times* reporter Mitchell Owens wrote in a 1997 article about Newark Museum's extensive exhibit that year. "It was outsourcing," he contended, "a form of production still practiced today."

Characterized by Owens as "avarice-inducing," the museum's exhibit featured such luxury items as sapphire-studded cuff links, aquamarine-encrusted lavalieres, gold mesh evening bags, silver spurs for horsewomen, and art nouveau dragonfly brooches set with diamonds. It is also important to note that many more mundane forms of jewelry, such as woven gold chains, belt buckles, gold bands and collar buttons, were also made in Newark.

Over the course of the nineteenth century, the United States transitioned from a country dependent on Europe for luxury goods to an internationally recognized manufacturing power. Income growth among Americans—a byproduct of the Industrial Revolution—was accompanied by a surging

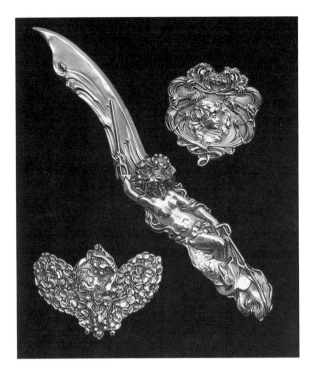

Belt buckles made by Unger Brothers (1872–1910), a Newark jewelry maker known for its sterling silver art nouveau designs. *Wikipedia.*

appetite for jewelry, one of a number of factors that contributed to Newark's success in the field. Another, of course, was its locale. The city's proximity to New York, as well as to Port Newark, rail links and, ultimately, Newark International Airport, supported widespread distribution of Newark-made goods.

In addition, two national events that occurred in the 1840s—a nearly 40 percent tariff on imported silver imposed by Congress as part of the sweeping Tariff Act in 1842, and the discovery of gold in California in 1848—greatly helped to reshape the U.S. jewelry market. The midcentury gold rush, as well as domestic manufacturers' innovation in accommodating the growing demand for fine jewelry, bolstered Americans' acceptance of ornamental pieces that were city-made.

Another thing in Newark's favor was the high regard in which its jewelry wholesalers and retailers were held for both their honesty and quality. Taylor & Baldwin, the city's early jewelry manufacturers, played a key role in that regard, frequently boasting of the fair dealing and superior workmanship of Newark's jewelers. The expectation of high quality went a long way in overcoming not only a prejudice against products made in Newark but also a disdain often extended to most American-made goods.

Newark jewelry makers also racked up a number of technological achievements that further enhanced their reputation. Pennington, Carter & Doremus, a city-based firm founded in 1841, earned acclaim as one of the first jewelry makers in the United States to use a steam engine. Some twenty-five years after purchasing the device from a Newark-based inventor in the 1850s, the firm—by then reconfigured as Carter, Howkins & Sloan—was purported to be the largest jewelry manufacturer in the world!

Ferdinand J. Herpers, one of Newark's many jewelry makers of German descent, earned a place in history as the designer of a new setting for diamond rings. He was awarded a patent for the design in 1872. Popularly known as the prong setting, the design features nearly invisible prongs used to prop up the diamond and better show off its brilliance. The prong setting, still in vogue today, went a long way in helping to secure the metropolitan area's prominence as a diamond center.

And there was more. Newark became a leader in smelting, largely thanks to one man, a German immigrant by the name of Edward Balbach. In 1865, Balbach patented his invention of "a new and improved process of separating silver and gold from lead." His precious-metal retrieval system provided an efficient means of collecting and processing the valuable sweepings from factory floors.

Late in the 1800s, the Newark firm Baker & Co became a national leader in the platinum and smelting business. By the turn of the century, Newark Museum's Sweeney Price wrote, platinum had undergone a surge in popularity, and the city's ability to process the precious metal easily gave it a decided edge. Precious metals, she wrote in the foreword to *The Glitter & the Gold*, were now accessible to the middle class.

No story about Newark as the one-time jewelry capital of the nation would be complete without highlighting the collar button, used by affluent men throughout the nineteenth and well into the twentieth century to fasten detachable shirt collars. "This is an odd moment where jewelry and clothing get close," Dietz stated. Although jewelry manufacturers made collar buttons, he noted that these items—like cuff links, buttons and shirt studs—are fasteners rather than ornaments.

George Krementz, who opened a jewelry-making company in Newark in 1866, perfected the design of a one-piece collar button: a button-sized stud consisting of a disk joined by a shank to a smaller shaft, for which he was awarded a patent in 1884. The design became so popular that at one time, Krementz & Co. made more than one million collar buttons annually. As the late Newark historian Charles Cummings wrote in a *Star-*

Ledger column in 1997, "99 percent of all American collar buttons were made right here in Newark."

The city's jewelry industry continued to thrive until the 1920s. Then came a recession early in the decade, followed by the stock market crash of 1929—the final death knell. "Gold jewelry and precious stones," Cummings wrote—which had been largely accessible to middle-class consumers— "were no match for unemployment lines and the near-desperation that faced many after the Wall Street crash." The Great Depression destroyed not only the jewelry industry but also the economy as a whole. In the first year alone, some two hundred Newark factories shut their doors.

Slowly, inexorably, costume jewelry—once referred to as "cheap jewelry," not as a slur but simply to emphasize that it was inexpensive—gained in popularity. Leading fashion designers, most notably Coco Chanel and Elsa Schiaparelli, began promoting "fake jewelry," Dietz recalled. And, as this type of jewelry was both fashionable and affordable, the populace embraced it. Another thing costume jewelry had in its favor, Dietz pointed out, was its accessibility. After all, "You could buy it at Woolworth's."

5
CENTURIES OF CIDER

E very autumn, orchards and farm stands that dot the Garden State
feature everything apple: apple butter, apple pies, applesauce, apple
cider and apple cider donuts—an overabundance of apples. In total,
New Jersey boasts more than thirty apple varieties, some of the best of which
have Newark roots.

Shortly after its founding in 1666, the settlement acquired a reputation
for top-notch cider. At one time, Newark History Society president Timothy
Crist said in a talk titled "Newark's Celebrated Cider and the Apples That
Made It Famous," Newark and the rest of Essex County—all initially part
of a single settlement—"were celebrated more for their orchards and apple
cider than for anything else."

The absence of safe drinking water was a major reason for cider's
importance in the settlement's early days. Cider was produced in numerous
settlements. But, says Charles Rosen, CEO of Ironbound Farm and
Ciderhouse, a "regenerative farm" that re-created Newark cider in the
twenty-first century, "Newark cider was the granddaddy of them all."

Historic records dating from just a few years after the Puritans arrived
in Newark echo the importance of cider, leaving little doubt that the drink
was a basic necessity. The Puritans either brought "apple scions" with them
from their New Haven colony or went back for them soon after, Crist noted.
Grafting branches or cuttings from trees with a desired apple variety onto
other trees typically ensures that the prized fruit will be reproduced.

As early as 1673, a mere seven years after the Puritans disembarked on the banks of the Passaic River, the cider owned by one Matthew Canfield was considered vital enough to be included in an inventory of his estate. Indeed, the Canfield apple, a high-quality variety that is now part of a three-apple mix used to produce Ironbound Hard Cider, shares his family name.

Further evidence of the abundance of orchards comes from a listing of a property acquired in 1678 by Abraham Pierson Jr., the second minister of Old First Church. In addition to the main dwelling, the document made clear, the sale had included a barn, a well, a yard, a garden and an orchard.

Apple orchards were vital as a source not only of the cider that entire families depended on but also of income. Records show evidence of a successful cider trade as early as the 1680s, when one early trader

Newark Cider Royal, a specialty of Ironbound Farm and Ciderhouse. *Brittany Ramaglia, courtesy of Ironbound Farm.*

raved about "the abundance of good Cyder, especially at a town called Newark which is esteemed at New York and other places where it is sold."

Nearly a century later, records show, David Ogden, a New Jersey Supreme Court justice whom Crist identified as "perhaps the best-known Newark resident at the time," owned an eleven-acre tract that he described as being "in high cultivation with a valuable orchard." Because Ogden was a Loyalist, however, his property was seized by the Patriots and the proceeds used to support the American Revolution.

Accolades continued throughout the eighteenth century.

In 1794, William Strickland, a prominent British farmer who stopped off in Newark en route to New York, wrote about the settlement in a travel journal. He liked Newark, observing that both the houses and the lay of the land reminded him of England. But he was especially taken with its orchards, which, he declared, "are said to produce the best Cyder in the US." A few years later, a property listing by one Elias Baldwin boasted that the sale included "an apple orchard of the best fruit."

Even George Washington, whose home state of Virginia turned out high-quality cider, was not immune. Presented with Newark cider as a gift from a judge late in the eighteenth century, Washington is said to have expressed a preference for it over the Virginian variety.

While growing and harvesting apples required a considerable effort over many months, cider making itself was a seasonable task. As a result, enterprising individuals often acquired and operated cider mills as a sideline to handily supplement their income.

The prices mills charged varied greatly, depending on the extent of the effort required. A mill owned by Samuel Harrison—the grandson of one of Newark's founders and whose family name is synonymous with what would become Newark's most prized apple—listed the following charges, circa 1740:

- Three pence per barrel for those who brought their own apples and did the work themselves but used Harrison's equipment to mill and press them into cider.
- One shilling per barrel for those who provided the apples but hired Harrison to do the work (twelve pence equaled one shilling).
- Eleven to thirteen shillings per barrel when Harrison both provided the apples and made the cider. (The sum roughly equaled what a laborer could earn in three days.)

In the decades that followed, the cider-making business appears to have exploded, as estimates of quantities produced in 1810 by a teacher and cider mill owner named Joseph W. Camp suggest. In early September, Camp began with about 600 bushels of apples per day. Two months later, the daily count exceeded 1,350 bushels. Over the course of the fall harvest that year, the mill processed more than 12,250 bushels of apples and had a total output of 1,200 barrels of cider. While Crist emphasized that the 1810 harvest appears to have been especially good, it is also true that these quantities reflect the output of only one of a large number of local cider mills. Not surprisingly, then, both the barrels in which the cider was stored and the cider itself were soon in hot demand.

Some cider was set aside for distilling into "cider spirits," later commonly called applejack. At the same time, some crafty entrepreneurs found that they could maximize their profits by turning fermented cider into a bubbly "champagne"—or *shampagne*, as one critic dubbed it.

Ethics notwithstanding, the price differential between ordinary cider and the sparkling variety passed off as champagne was large enough to be extremely tempting. Fran McManus, a food writer and cultural strategist for Ironbound Farm, who shared the podium with Crist at the Newark History Society talk on Newark cider, reported that in 1873, ordinary cider might sell for about $6 a barrel, or roughly 20 cents a gallon, while the same quantity of the bubbly beverage could fetch somewhere around $360.

Today, one of the products produced by Ironbound Farm is a sparkling cider. An anecdote on its website (ironboundhardcider.com) harkens back to the nineteenth century with a quote dating from the 1840s by Scottish-born journalist Alexander Mackay: "Many is the American connoisseur of champagne who has his taste cultivated on Newark cider." This observation was reinforced, the story goes, when Mackay encountered a New Yorker who described Newark as "the great champagne manufactory of America."

The fact that apple cider could so easily be converted into a drink that resembled champagne is further evidence of the high quality of Newark cider apples. The taste was so good that one observer reported that not only did the country's best cider come from Newark but so did a majority of its best champagne.

What accounted for the richness of Newark cider? The answer lies mainly in the apples themselves. But, as an orchardist who attempted without success to reproduce Newark's finest in Ohio discovered, the secret lies in the red, rocky soil found throughout much of Essex County. The same apples, when grown in Ohio, could not compare.

Starting in the early 1700s, one variety stood out from the rest: the Harrison apple. Small, yellow, long-stemmed and flecked with distinctive black dots, it was described as rich, spicy and complex. Harrison apple beverages were also known to have a higher alcohol content than other varieties.

Originally found in a part of greater Newark that is now South Orange, the apple tree—first given the name Osborne for the owner of the property on which it was found—was later among a variety of young grafted trees passed on to Samuel Harrison. As is already evident in the description of his cider mill's price structure, Harrison was an enterprising entrepreneur. And while it is likely that he followed the popular custom of giving cuttings from high-quality apple trees to friends and family, it is worth noting as well that in the first few decades of the nineteenth century, cider from Harrison apples sold for four to five times as much as cider made in New England.

While Harrison trees proliferated through much of the eighteenth and nineteenth centuries, as the twentieth century approached, both the apple itself and the cider business began to wane. The temperance movement may have contributed to a decline in cider sales. But increasing industrialization

Small, yellow and flecked with black dots, the Harrison apple has been recognized for its superior taste for centuries. *Brittany Ramaglia, courtesy of Ironbound Farm.*

and less farmland played a role, too, as did cider's reputation as an unsophisticated drink popular mainly in rural America among a less well-to-do and less educated populace.

In time, Harrison trees fell victim to insect infestation, a problem exacerbated by mismanagement. But, as McManus said in her lecture, the popular belief at the time was that apple varieties had a finite life span. Thus, the role of orchardists in contributing to the demise of the Harrison tree was largely overlooked.

Ultimately, the Harrison apple went missing for the better part of a century. That might have been the end of the line had it not been for a determined "apple hunter" by the name of Paul Gidez, a Vermont farmer who traversed New Jersey in search of the Harrison tree. In 1976, a conversation with a local resident at a Livingston bagel shop led Gidez to the site of an old cider mill, where he spotted a solitary Harrison tree.

Gidez took cuttings back to his farm in Vermont, but the man who gets the bulk of the credit for bringing back the Harrison apple was a Virginian named Tom Burford. A fifth-generation orchardist, Burford—whom Charles Rosen of Ironbound Farm and Ciderhouse hails as "one of the world's foremost authorities on historic American apple cultivars"—was known to many as "Professor Apple."

Burford, who passed away in 2020, was floored when he first tasted the Harrison apple. He could not imagine why such an amazing apple had been allowed to wither away, McManus told attendees at the Newark History Society lecture on the city's cider industry. The Harrison apple, Burford declared, was "the most enigmatic apple" he had ever encountered.

Rosen secured his first hundred Harrison trees from Burford. The trees formed the basis for the Asbury, New Jersey orchard that supplies Ironbound Farm's cider house. And, Rosen says proudly, "we ended up with ten thousand in the ground."

The farm, which practices what Rosen describes as "regenerative agriculture," has passed on the tradition, giving some 2,500 young Harrison trees to an upstate New York farm. Besides helping to support other small family farms, ensuring that Harrison trees are grown in various locales serves additional purposes. It allows horticulturists to take a closer measure of the effects of soil on the apples themselves, and it increases the likelihood that this unique variety of apple will continue to thrive.

Part of Rosen's original intent in opening Ironbound Farm and Ciderhouse was to support Newark and its residents. He originally wanted to establish the cider operation in the city, but a law requiring that such facilities have several adjacent acres of orchards prevented it, leading him to the Hunterdon County location instead.

Now, however, that law has been rescinded, and Rosen hopes to bring part of his cider works back to the city where many of his products got their start. He has begun working with the Newark Alliance and other community-development groups on ways to create a regional food system, and he plans on acquiring a Newark "cidery" license in order to bring cider making full circle.

6

NEWARK'S SHERLOCK TAKES ON RADIUM

In the beginning, the young women who worked for the Radium Luminous Materials Corporation in Newark adored their jobs. And for good reason. Most were young—the youngest hire was barely fifteen—and many were from immigrant families of little means. And all were well paid, some earning more than their fathers. Then, too, there was the entrancing glow, literally. The powder the women used to mix the luminescent glow-in-the-dark paint they applied to the numbers on watch faces ended up everywhere, making their clothes, their hair and even their bodies glimmer. For a time, they thought it was glamorous.

The fact that they were working with radium lent an added air of excitement. The element had been discovered by Marie Curie and her husband, Pierre, in 1898, less than twenty years before the company hired the women as dial painters. Radium was hailed as a "magnificent cure-all" and "the greatest find of history," author Kate Moore wrote in *The Radium Girls: The Dark Story of America's Shining Women*.

The book, published in 2017, quickly became a bestseller. Its little-known story is horrifying, its title apt. For the dial painters, a dark, even deadly reality slowly emerged as radium insidiously attacked their bodies. But first came the country's entrance into World War I in 1917, which brought with it a huge uptick in business for their employer.

With luminescent numbers needed on military equipment like airplane panels and submarine dials, as well as on clock faces and watches worn by American troops, the Newark headquarters proved to be too small to accommodate the additional staff needed to fill the surge in orders. So Radium Luminous closed its studio on Third Street and moved into a two-story building in a residential section of Orange just a short distance away. To keep up with the demand, the "radium girls," as they were later known, worked long hours. At times, they remained on the job seven days a week.

While Radium Luminous, later known as the US Radium Corporation (USRC), left Newark, the state's largest city and many of its residents were key players in the story that unfolded. Many radium girls lived in Newark, and a number of the doctors and dentists whose help they sought for their increasingly distressing symptoms practiced there. What's more, it was a lifelong Newarker—a pathologist named Harrison Martland, affectionately known as "Newark's Sherlock Holmes"—who worked tirelessly to pinpoint the source of their ailments. Dr. Martland, along with a Newark-based attorney by the name of Raymond Berry, did everything possible to see that the young women and their families received the recompense they deserved.

In 1927, after years as a staff pathologist at Newark City Hospital, Martland became Essex County medical examiner. He was the first to

Dial painters working at the US Radium Corporation. *Wikipedia.*

hold that position. Over the course of his career, Martland performed an estimated thirty thousand autopsies, more than one on a former dial painter whose death was the result of radium poisoning.

Looking back, the fact that oral ailments were among the first and most severe to surface among the radium girls should not have come as a surprise. That's because the women routinely used a method colloquially known as "lip, dip, paint." And that is exactly what they did.

The numerals on watch faces and dials were typically so minute that even with the fine camel-hair brushes the dial painters used, it was difficult if not impossible to paint with the required precision. What's more, as the women worked, the bristles on the brushes spread out. Lip-pointing was the recommended solution, a method virtually all the dial painters adopted.

Before almost every new application, a dial-painter would moisten the tip of the brush with her mouth to reshape the bristles into a point. When any of the women expressed concern about the practice, Moore reported, they were assured that lip-pointing was perfectly safe. The amount of radium used in the paint, company doctors asserted, was far too small to cause any harm.

By the early 1920s, however, reality flew in the face of that assertion. One by one, dial painters who had been on the job for more than a short time began to acquire severe pain and infection in the teeth and jaw, among other ailments. One dentist observed, with surprise, that long after he had pulled the tooth of a young patient, the socket failed to heal. Later, when he reached inside the young woman's mouth to investigate, he was shocked when a piece of her jawbone broke off in his hand.

Within a couple of years, enough dial painters exhibited similar symptoms that the syndrome acquired a name: jaw rot. But pinpointing the cause, or, more accurately, proving causation, remained elusive. One practitioner suspected phosphorous poisoning, but an analysis of the luminescent paint found that phosphorous was not one of the ingredients.

It turned out to be a chemist whom USRC hired to analyze the luminescent paint who first laid the blame on radium. In January 1923—even before conducting the tests he had planned—he wrote to the president of the corporation. "It is my belief that the serious condition of the jaw has been caused by the influence of radium," his letter stated. "There is good reason to fear that neglect of precautions may result in serious injury to the radium workers themselves," he went on, warning of "the dangers of getting this material on the skin or into the system, especially the mouth."

It is not clear what became of that letter. What is evident is that nothing changed, even when the chemist reiterated, after completing the tests several months later, "I feel quite sure that the opinion expressed in my former letter is correct."

Still, by early 1924, the president of USRC was threatened enough by reports of stricken dial painters and allegations of radium poisoning that he felt the need for a medical investigation. He turned to a professor at the Harvard School of Public Health who was both a pathologist and an established expert in occupational disease. Yet despite having sought a comprehensive review, when the final report was delivered, USRC whitewashed it. In summarizing the findings to the New Jersey Department of Labor, USRC highlighted a single table to falsely conclude that the radium girls were in the best of health. The state accepted the "evidence," allowing the corporation to dodge another bullet. Yet the reprieve proved to be short-lived.

Soon, several of the radium girls with the most severe conditions filed suit against USRC. Their impairments included joint pain significant enough to hinder movement and deterioration of the spine; red blood cell abnormalities that, while initially suggestive of excellent health, in time proved to be anemia; digestive and mouth problems that made eating difficult; and jaw necrosis. In the summer of 1927, Moore reported: "It became official. The Case of the Five Women Doomed to Die had now begun." Their lawsuits were consolidated into what was sometimes called "the case of the decade."

Enter Newark's Sherlock Holmes. Ironically, Dr. Martland teamed up with a man who had been at the helm of the radium corporation in its early days to find a way to conduct a definitive investigation. His name was Dr. Sabin von Sochocky.

Their work was twofold: to establish that radium was the cause of death in those who had passed away, and to prove that radium poisoning was responsible for the vast array of distressing symptoms afflicting those who had fallen ill but had not yet succumbed.

The first goal was achieved through exhumation. Martland and von Sochocky burned the bones of the cadavers until they turned to ash, then subjected the ashes to a device called an electrometer, which measured radioactivity in the body. The findings conclusively showed radium poisoning.

The bones of living victims of radium poisoning cannot be burned or pulverized, of course, so another means of measuring dial painters' exposure was needed. Martland and von Sochocky devised two ways of doing so. One was to use the same electrometer that measured radioactivity in the remains of the dead to measure radiation leakage from the bones of the living. This could be accomplished, they discovered, by holding the instrument close to a patient's chest. The other assessment tool involved breath analysis. Both measures found exceedingly high levels of radium in the severely ill woman who was the first to undergo this pair of tests. The same results were found in those who underwent subsequent testing, even when they were so weak they could barely move.

As the trial unfolded, these same women, some with voices so diminished they could scarcely be heard, were put on the witness stand to testify. One after another swore that she had routinely used lip-pointing, testifying that while they were provided an alternate means of cleansing and pointing the brushes for a short time, the medium used for this purpose was withdrawn before long because company officials found that it wasted too much of the radium paint. Multiple dial painters reported that their use of the lip, dip and paint method was widely known and even taught to them by their supervisors, while an officer of USRC insisted the method had never been used.

Martland, however—known to many as the trial's star witness—contradicted the officer's testimony and highlighted the evidence resulting from his method of verification. Walter Lippmann, the acclaimed journalist who wrote for the *World*—"arguably the most powerful newspaper in America" at the time, according to Moore—spoke out on behalf of the dial painters as well.

Before the case concluded, USRC sought a settlement. Each plaintiff would receive $10,000, the corporation proposed. This was a massive sum at the time. The catch was that under the terms USRC offered, both medical and litigation costs would be deducted. The plaintiffs, all of whom were doomed to death, refused.

The counteroffer was a $15,000 payout, along with numerous other provisions.

The terms finally agreed on included a $10,000 cash lump sum. In addition, each of the women would receive a $600 per year pension for life, and the corporation would cover all medical costs, both past and future, as well as court costs. While the settlement did not come with an admission of guilt, USRC was implicated in the court of public opinion.

Sadly, however, that was far from the end. The Radium Dial Company, based in Ottawa, Illinois, remained in operation well into the 1930s. During that time, the company continued to deny what its executives had been aware of at least since 1925, when the lawsuit began in New Jersey and

Martland's tests provided conclusive evidence of radium poisoning. Indeed, when news of the New Jersey case reached Ottawa in 1928, the company took out a full-page ad declaring that its radium paint was "pure" and safe. In Illinois, as in New Jersey a decade earlier, dial painting was a well-paying, highly sought job.

Then in 1934, as more radium girls were stricken with illness and death, a large group of dial painters filed suit, seeking a payout of $50,000 apiece. That case was lost, largely based on the argument that the plaintiffs had exceeded the statute of limitations. But a single plaintiff, testifying within days of her demise, prevailed. Radium Dial appealed, but to no avail. The plaintiff, who weighed less than sixty pounds in her final days, died in July 1938.

Ultimately, though, she and the other young women who fought so long and hard for justice had a huge impact. As Moore noted, they did not die in vain. Within days of the conclusion of the Ottawa trial, World War II broke out in Europe. With it came the same high demand for luminous dials that World War I had wrought. But gone were the days when radium companies had free rein.

"Safety standards were introduced that protected a whole new generation of dial painters," Moore concluded. The courage and advocacy of the young women who came before them led to radioactivity protections in the workplace that no doubt saved thousands of lives.

PART III

NOTABLE FIRSTS

7

PATENT LEATHER AND BEYOND

Countless American girls who grew up proudly sporting patent leather "Mary Janes" with their Sunday-best outfits owe a note of thanks to an indomitable Newark-based inventor by the name of Seth Boyden. Hailed by none other than Thomas Edison as "one of America's greatest inventors" and known to some as "the [Henry] Ford of Newark," Boyden nonetheless failed to patent his means of creating the product whose very name identifies it as a patentable process.

Seth Boyden was the first American to develop a means of transforming animal hides into the high-sheen, water-resistant, ornamental patent leather. And he was the first to open a factory for that purpose. Patent leather existed overseas, however, long before Boyden was old enough to envision it.

One of ten children, Seth Boyden Jr. was born in Foxborough, Massachusetts, in 1788. When he was five years old, an article in the British *Literary Weekly Intelligencer* (aka *The Bee)* mentioned "Hand's patent leather." A man by the name of Hand, the 1793 article stated, had obtained a patent for providing "flexible leather" with a shiny, protective coating that "renders it impervious to water." References to a "glazed ornamental leather invented in France" can also be found. From the time Boyden first encountered European-style patent leather, though, he was determined to make a similar but superior high-sheen leather of his own.

Boyden came from a family of innovators. His grandfather had an iron foundry. His father, Seth Sr., worked as both a farmer and a blacksmith and designed a leather-splitting machine said to be capable of carving animal hides into whatever thickness was desired. What the *New York Times* hailed as his son Seth's "mechanical genius" was evident from an early age.

When he was still in his teens, Seth Boyden built both a telescope and a microscope. He soon became known for his skill in repairing clocks and guns. By the time he was twenty-one, Boyden was making nails, tacks, brads and cutting files, using machinery he built himself to improve production. Before long, he had devised a way of enhancing his father's leather-splitting process as well.

Boyden's interest in tanneries was what led him to Newark, where leather was one of the most lucrative industries. In or around 1813, he moved to the city with his brother to set up shop. The precision of the leather-splitting process Boyden had perfected made it possible to slice sheepskin and leather thin enough for use in bookbinding. Boyden's business model achieved rapid success. But he was a tireless tinkerer, always looking for new things to invent or processes to perfect. Soon, patent leather caught his eye.

On a trip to New York in 1818, Seth Boyden spotted a German military cap, its leather visor so stiff and shiny that it appeared to be heavily lacquered. Intrigued, he set out to find a way to achieve a similar effect. Described by author Brad Tuttle in *How Newark Became Newark* as a "gentle, inquisitive character who conducted experiments at all hours of the night and day," Boyden did a reverse engineering of sorts. Barely taking time to bathe or change his clothes, he tried out a series of glossy finishes until he found a formula that yielded the look and feel he sought.

The patent leather Boyden ultimately developed retained the sheen and the water-resistant properties of the European product. But it had one significant advantage. Instead of the stiff and brittle feel of the visor that had triggered Boyden's frenzied experiments, his patent leather was far more pliable.

Boyden's formula used linseed oil as varnish. To achieve the finished product, a hide was stretched on a wooden frame, and then coat after coat of the oil was applied, with the leather allowed to dry after each successive layer. Once it had the desired look and feel, the coating was baked on.

In 1819, Boyden opened the nation's first patent leather factory. Like his leather-splitting plant before it, this manufacturing enterprise quickly caught on. Patent leather, particularly valued for the dressy look it lent to shoes and boots, was sought after for use in harnesses and carriages as well.

Although Boyden's business boomed, his failure to patent the American patent leather formula made it easy for others to follow his lead. In 1837, less than twenty years after Boyden opened his own patent leather factory, more than 150 other Newark manufacturers were producing it. By 1860, Tuttle reported, "Newark was responsible for 90 percent of all patent leather made in the United States."

Boyden next turned his attention to iron. Having observed that the frequent heating required to turn iron ore into desired shapes had an adverse effect on its durability, he devised what a metallurgic engineer described as "a two-step heat treatment method" to produce a malleable product.

Getting to that point, however, involved lengthy experiments, which often required that a fire continue to burn for days at a time. So Boyden slept in his clothes and jerry-rigged what Tuttle described as a makeshift alarm. He affixed a candle to the wall, setting it up so that when the candle burned down sufficiently, it would fall off the wall and plop into a container. The noise that resulted was loud enough to awaken the sleeping inventor, thereby ensuring that he would be up in time to tend the fire.

The iron that Boyden ultimately produced was sufficiently soft and pliable while maintaining its resilience. Dubbed "malleable iron"—the first of its kind in the United States—it met Boyden's criteria: that it be "cheaper than wrought iron, less brittle than cast iron, and more malleable than both."

Having achieved his goal, Boyden sold off his patent leather plant and opened a malleable iron foundry—another national first for the prolific inventor. Caring more about helping the workingman than enriching himself, Boyden once again neglected to apply for a patent. He did receive a prominent award from Philadelphia's Franklin Institute for his malleable iron castings, but gunsmiths, locksmiths, blacksmiths and coach makers were the primary beneficiaries.

Boyden went on to design a locomotive capable of mounting the steep grades west of Newark, thereby solving a problem that had stymied the rail industry until it made its maiden journey in 1837. He is said to have worked with Samuel Morse on the telescope and is credited with producing the first daguerreotype in the United States.

And there's more. Boyden built steam engines and custom-built a steam fire truck for Newark. When city commissioners complained about the cost of curving elbow joints in the steam pipes, Boyden is said to have retorted, "God, in all his works, never made a right angle."

His design of a cut-off valve for steam engines is considered by many to be his most important invention. Not surprisingly, he did not patent that, either. Despite his numerous innovations, Boyden filed only one patent application. Awarded in 1860, the patent was for "machinery for hardening

A bronze statue of Seth Boyden standing alongside an anvil and a hammer was dedicated in 1890. *Wikimedia Commons.*

hat-bodies." The National Inventors Hall of Fame, which inducted Boyden in 2006, described the device as a "hat-forming machine."

Seth Boyden's reluctance to seek formal recognition for his work goes a long way to explain why he remained relatively unknown by the general public. Some people who grew up in Newark or its nearby suburbs may be aware that he was the first to produce patent leather in the United States. Others know of him only through places that bear his name, such as the Seth Boyden public housing project in Newark's South Ward. In Maplewood, where he spent his final years, both an avenue and an elementary school are named for him.

Still others will have seen the statue of Seth Boyden. He is depicted standing, clad in a mechanic's apron and at work at an anvil, in a park across from the Newark Museum of Art. The park was known until 2022 as Washington Park, when Newark mayor Ras Baraka announced a name change to Harriet Tubman Square.

Unveiled in May 1890, the Boyden statue may have been the first to honor the workingman. A plaque on its base calls Boyden a "pioneer in mechanics" and "benefactor of industry." It also states, "His inventive faculty led him far afield into art, physics, chemistry, horticulture and botany." His interest in horticulture took center stage in his later years, when he turned his attention to the cultivation of local strawberries. Through experimentation with hybridization, he developed bigger and plumper varieties of the fruit, given names like the Boyden, the Hilton, the Green Prolific and others.

An article by a Maplewood garden club noted that, because the normal process of producing strawberry seeds took so long, Boyden found a way to speed it up by adding a freezing mixture to the soil—thus doing "in 48 hours what typically would take all winter." Rather than make money on this process, Boyden gave strawberry plants to all his friends and neighbors.

The obituary of Boyden that appeared in the *New York Times* on April 1, 1870, aptly summed up his accomplishments: "During all his life, this remarkable man, whose inventions have made millions for others, was himself, poor, but his poverty was forgotten in his genial spirits and his noble life. Up to the latest days of his life, the thoughts that had accompanied him from early manhood and that had accomplished so many beneficial results, were still working after further discoveries; his intellect as clear and his spirits as ambitious as ever."

8

BIRTH OF THE BEER CAN

No one knows for sure when or how beer originated or evolved, but none doubt that it has been in existence for thousands of years. Although the first barley beer has been traced to the Sumerians of ancient Mesopotamia, it has long since been popular throughout the world.

Globally, more beer is consumed than any other alcoholic beverage—and beer is widely reported to be the third-most-popular drink of any kind, topped only by tea and water. So it should come as no surprise that shortly after Newark was founded in 1666, beer followed.

Beer was "the vital liquid that powered Newark's residents from its earliest years," Daniel Kurz wrote in a 2013 *Newark Patch* post. Part of the reason was that in colonial Newark, which began as a Puritan theocracy, the tavern was the main gathering place—other than church—and offered more opportunity for residents to discuss politics, exchange gossip and kick back and relax. But Kurz points to another crucial reason for early Newarkers' immediate embrace of beer: It was far safer to drink than water.

Although the beer the colonists consumed did not have a high alcohol content, it was sufficient to kill the "deadly microbes, tiny insects and other invisible enemies" found in water, Kurz noted. "In the 1700s and 1800s," he concluded, "if you were thirsty anywhere in Newark, and you had a brain in your head, you drank beer." (Cider was wildly popular for the same reason and, indeed, may even have predated beer as early Newarkers' beverage of choice.)

As Newark transitioned from an agrarian colonial community to a rapidly growing industrial hub, brewing became one of the city's most important industries. From 1849 to 1958, the late Newark historian Charles Cummings wrote, "Newark went from a town where the local brewmaster carried hops in a wheelbarrow to one of the nation's and the world's largest brewing centers." By the 1880s, Newark had twenty-six breweries that collectively produced some 420,000 barrels of beer annually. A mere ten years later, the yearly output topped 2,000,000 barrels.

Newark breweries thrived in part because of the city's metropolitan locale, with easy access to transportation of all kinds. Then, too, there was a ready workforce, including a steady input of immigrants, many of whom had mastered beer production in their mother countries. Of vital importance, too, was the quality of Newark's water, beginning in the late nineteenth century. Joseph G. Haynes, mayor of Newark from 1884 until 1894, funded the city's watershed in Sussex, Passaic and Morris Counties, ensuring long-term access to water that was high in quality, plentiful and inexpensive.

A handful of the city's brewers became millionaires, building grand mansions within city limits and becoming civic leaders. The best known home to modern-day residents is the Ballantine House, the elegant brownstone that has since been incorporated into the Newark Museum of Art. But another brewer—Krueger—holds a special place in beer history as the first to put the beloved beverage into cans.

In 1858, Gottfried Krueger, a young German immigrant, arrived here when he was just sixteen. He came to Newark for the express purpose of working with his uncle, John Laible, to cofound the Gottfried Krueger Brewing Company. A few years later, Krueger partnered with a man named Gottlieb Hill to purchase an existing brewery, renaming it Hill & Krueger. The business thrived, and when Hill passed away, Krueger changed its name to G. Krueger Brewing Company.

In the years leading up to Prohibition, which took effect in 1920, American Can Company had begun experimenting with packaging beer in cans. The company sought a brewer to partner with, but Prohibition forced it to put the plan on hold.

While some brewers shut down their operations at the time, Krueger continued production, both of soft drinks and of near beer (0.5 percent alcohol), which was still legal. Thus, in 1933, when it became clear that the amendment authorizing Prohibition would be overturned before the end of the year, Krueger was ready. American Can offered to install equipment needed to put beer in cans inside the Krueger plant. And the can company

Krueger's introduced the beer can in 1933. *Courtesy of Beer Can Collectors of America.*

agreed not to charge the brewery if its canned beer didn't sell, thereby giving G. Krueger all the incentive it needed. So it was that in late 1933, just before the official end of Prohibition, two thousand cans filled with Krueger's "Special Beer"—containing 3.2 percent alcohol—rolled off the assembly line.

Even with American Can's promises, the brewer held back, distributing this first run of canned beer only to employees, families and friends, lest the concept fail miserably. Krueger needn't have worried. Almost all of those who tried the "Special Beer"—a whopping 91 percent—gave it a thumbs-up.

As a self-described "lighthearted documentary" titled *Beer Can: A Love Story* (https://beercanalovestory.com) makes clear, cans have a number of practical benefits over bottles. They're stackable, more compact and lighter than glass and unbreakable. That makes them easier and cheaper to transport and allows beer drinkers to store larger quantities in both the fridge and the cooler. What's more, while both glass bottles and the aluminum cans that beer now comes in require recycling, at the time, bottles required deposits that were returned when they were brought back. Cans did not.

But what of the taste? The steel cans that beer originally was packaged in had a liner, designed to prevent leaching or rusting and ensure that the beverage did not acquire a metallic tinge. How well it worked was subject to debate. Nonetheless, the Brewery Collectibles Club of America (BCCA) reports that 85 percent of those who tried Krueger's first foray into canned beer said it tasted more like draft than bottled beer.

The success of the test run prompted Krueger to sell canned beer. On January 24, 1935, a date that looms large in the minds of many beer aficionados, the brewery brought to market cans of two brands of its full-strength beer, Krueger's Cream Ale and Krueger's Finest Beer. But early success notwithstanding, Gottfried Krueger was cautious. The brewery shipped the cans to its farthest distributor, in Richmond, Virginia. If the canned beer did not catch on, Krueger hoped the failure would not affect its metropolitan market.

Once again, he needn't have worried. Canned beer was a smashing success. By the summer of 1935, an article in *Wired* magazine reports, "Krueger was buying 180,000 cans a day from American Can"—a growth spurt of a whopping 550 percent!

Today, Krueger's early beer cans are highly prized collectors' items. The graphic features a stick man shaped like the letter *K*. Affectionately known as "K-man," the elegantly clad figure appears to be a waiter bearing a tray with a can and a glass. In the initial runs, K-man's head is uncovered. Sometime after, he acquired a rounded cap, reminiscent of a porter or a character in an early cigarette ad. To collectors, those without hats are known as "baldies."

The unexpected popularity of canned beer prompted a number of other breweries, including Northampton Brewery, Schlitz and a few beer sellers overseas, to quickly follow suit. Many others, particularly makers of higher-end and premium imported beers, vowed to stand firm. Canned beer, they contended, was the province of the working man. The battle of the bottle and the can was just beginning.

Beer Can: A Love Story playfully traces the struggle. Featuring one man dressed as a can and another as a bottle, the video highlights the "can's rise to prominence in the mid-twentieth century, rapid fall with the birth of the craft beer movement and newfound modern resurrection."

Beer can design, like attitudes about the cans, has undergone a number of changes in the nearly ninety years since canned beer was first sold. The earliest cans, known as flat tops, required the device popularly known as a church key to pry them open.

Cone-top cans, which had funnel-like tops more reminiscent of beer bottles, soon appeared. They were favored, according to BCCA, by smaller brewers, because the cone tops made it possible for the cans to be filled by the same equipment as that used for bottled beer. A downside of the cone top, of course, was that the cans weren't stackable.

Next came the self-opening can, introduced by the Pittsburgh Brewing Company in the early 1960s. By 1965, BCCA reports, some 70 percent of beer cans had tab-top openers. Environmentally, though, the pull tabs were a disaster. They ended up everywhere. Animals ingested them and died, kids cut their feet on them on beaches and beer drinkers themselves occasionally choked on the tabs.

The result? A decade after the introduction of the pull-tab tops, the stay tab—now used on virtually every canned beverage on the market—came into being. Along the way, the makeup of the can itself changed, from heavy-gauge coated steel to a lightweight and rust-resistant aluminum.

As longtime holdouts for bottles began to embrace canned beer in recent years, many claimed that the metallic taste long attributed to beer packaged in cans had ceased to be a problem. Some say there never was a metallic taste, while others believe that better design led to better taste.

What is clear to virtually everyone is that the beer can has come out ahead. Pre-COVID, some 60 percent of the beer consumed in the United States was canned. And as the number of microbreweries continues to grow and small brewers are increasingly turning to canned beer, its lead is growing.

Today, the Brewers Association reports, beer in the United States is a more than $100 billion industry. And although beer sales rose by just 1 percent in 2021—the latest year for which figures are available—craft brewery sales grew 8 percent, "raising small and independent brewers' share of the U.S. beer market by volume to 13.1%."

January 24 is known as National Beer Can Appreciation Day, highlighted on the website nationaltoday.com with a timeline. The year 1969, it proclaims, marked the first time sales of canned beer topped that of bottled beer. It also denotes three reasons why we love National Beer Can Appreciation Day: Cans take less time to chill, are easier to stack—indeed, stacking beer bottles may indeed be impossible—and are more durable. "The advent of canned beer allowed U.S. brewers to ship millions of cans of beer to soldiers overseas during World War II," the website announces, before raving about beer cans' other attributes. They can "float a river, summit a mountain, and shred the gnar"—a term used in sports such as skateboarding, skiing and snowboarding to indicate performing well under a variety of difficult terrains—"all while staying pressurized, delicious and ready when you are."

What bottle can do that?

9

Introducing the County Park

From a historical perspective, Branch Brook Park holds a place of national distinction. Established in 1895, it was the first county park in the United States. Situated on Newark's north side, it was developed under the auspices of the Essex County Park Commission—a national first of its own.

Sprawling over 360 acres and stretching beyond Newark's border into neighboring Belleville, Branch Brook Park also has a twenty-first-century distinction: It is home to more than 5,200 Japanese cherry trees of more than eighteen varieties, producing the largest and arguably the most dazzling cherry blossom display in the country. Essex County Executive Joseph DiVincenzo Jr. once boasted in an interview that Branch Brook's collection of ornamental blossoms is larger and more diverse than that of any other site in the world.

Every April, some ten thousand people attend Newark's Cherry Blossom Festival. But few are aware of the festival's place in history. Whether they hail from Newark, the surrounding suburbs or farther afield, the vast majority of those who come to ooh and aah over the stunning array of dusty rose, pale pink and snowy white blossoms that blanket the area for a few weeks each year do not know that it all began with a generous gift to the park nearly a century ago.

Branch Brook Park has yet another distinction. Besides being the first park developed by the Essex County Park Commission, it is the county's largest. Weequahic Park, in Newark's South Ward, is next in line, with more than

Branch Brook Park, established in 1895, is home to more than five thousand Japanese cherry trees. *NewarkHappening.com.*

311 acres. It, too, was developed in the final years of the nineteenth century. And, like Branch Brook Park, Weequahic Park holds a place or two in history.

One distinction is its name. Weequahic, a derivative of the Lenni Lenape word for "head of the creek," is the only Native American word attached to a place in the city. At first, the name *Weequahic* referred only to the eighty-acre lake—Essex County's largest—that was later incorporated into the park. In time, the park adopted the name. Eventually, Weequahic became the name of the section of the city in which the park is located, a street (Weequahic Avenue) within the district and the art deco school (Weequahic High) built in 1932.

In precolonial days, Weequahic Lake is believed to have served as a dividing line between the Hackensack and Raritan factions of the Lenni Lenape Indians. When European settlers began laying claim to the land in the seventeenth century, the lake formed a natural boundary between Newark and Elizabethtown. The park is renowned for the horse racing that took place on its grounds both before and after its development. The races began in the mid-1800s and continued, all told, for the better part of a century.

Besides being the two largest parks in Essex County, Branch Brook and Weequahic have other common bonds.

The grounds of both once served the military. Camp Frelinghuysen, a training ground and encampment for several regiments during the Civil War, would decades later become part of Branch Brook. During World War II at Weequahic Park, the racetrack was turned into a military hospital and horse racing ceased. Barracks were erected in Weequahic Park for the military as well, and the buildings—divided into units that included two bedrooms, a living room and a kitchen—continued to house families of returning veterans until the early 1950s.

Both Branch Brook Park and the Weequahic Park Historic District are in the National Register of Historic Places.

Both were developed by the storied landscape architecture firm of Frederick Law Olmsted, the man most famous for designing New York's Central Park.

A timeline compiled by the Branch Brook Park Alliance highlights a visit by Olmsted in 1867, when Newarkers sought help in locating an ideal spot for a municipal park. Olmsted and his partner suggested a site on which Branch Brook Park would eventually be developed, the alliance notes. They envisioned it becoming Newark's "grand central park," a vision that "embodied their view that all people, regardless of their position in society, were entitled to fresh air, quiet places and the beauty that only nature can provide."

Some thirty years later, that vision was on its way to becoming a reality. On land donated by the Newark Aqueduct Board plus adjacent acreage gifted by some of Newark's most prominent families, the newly formed Essex County Park Commission hired two men to design and oversee Branch Brook's development.

The initial design was "gardenesque," featuring geometrically patterned gardens and an abundance of ornamental arbors, viaducts, gazebos and the like. The transformation of the grounds was well underway when the park commissioners realized that this was not quite what they had in mind. So, in 1898, they turned to the Olmsted firm.

Olmsted's descendants, who now led the firm, submitted a design with a far more naturalistic style, reflecting the vision they had inherited from the senior Olmsted. But because some of the gardenesque design had already been implemented, the Olmsteds had little choice but to let it be.

But how to move on? What could be done to merge such drastic differences in style? The creative solution to this dilemma was to divide the park into thirds.

The first, most southerly division incorporated the elaborate, carefully sculpted look that the former landscape designers had implemented.

The middle division would function as a transitional zone in which both indigenous and exotic plants intermingled. And the northern division, which is the largest, would be the most naturalistic part of the park.

Nonetheless, referring to Branch Brook Park's northern division as naturalistic may be a tad deceiving. Its gently flowing contours and green fields belie its predevelopment natural state, which was aptly described as "scruffy wet lowlands" incorporating a "dismal marsh" popularly known as Old Blue Jay Swamp. Shortly after its transformation, the northern part of the park began attracting thousands of visitors every autumn for a chrysanthemum show that endured for some seventy years.

In Branch Brook Park's early decades, donations continued unabated. Indeed, in 1927, Caroline Bamberger Fuld—the sister of department store magnate Louis Bamberger and wife of his partner, Felix Fuld—announced the gift that would do more than any other to attract crowds and put the park on the map: two thousand ornamental cherry trees.

Fuld, an avid traveler, was taken by the splendor of the cherry blossom groves she had seen in Washington, D.C., and hoped to replicate it in Newark. But the trees did not arrive in the park for some time. Fuld, an avid gardener, nurtured the trees at her estate in Orange, New Jersey, until they had grown enough to be ready for transplantation.

The trees were put into the northern part of the park, but another area—dubbed the extension division—was developed to accommodate them. With guidance from the Olmsteds, the cherry trees were laid out on tiered slopes overlooking a river valley. The designers aimed to replicate the way the magnificent cherry blossoms were seen in Japan.

It took many more years for the trees to mature. As one local historian put it, "It wasn't until the 1940s that the cherry blossoms really came into their own." And it wasn't until 1976 that the Newark Cherry Blossom Festival was officially established. Ever since, Cherryblossomland draws huge crowds every April as visitors flock to the park to bask in the beauty, picnic amid the blossoms, listen to music and participate in everything from bike races to fun runs. Visitors can enjoy a self-guided cellphone tour and use the Bloomwatch Webcam (http://ecpo2.packetalk.net:5350/IVC/views.htm#) to plan a visit when the blossoms are at their peak.

Cherry blossom peeping, of course, is just one of a large array of activities to enjoy at Branch Brook Park. A 4.6-mile trail known as the Branch Brook Park Loop attracts runners, hikers, bikers and walkers year-round. Tennis courts, athletic fields, a dog park, a skating rink, a playground and bocce courts are among the many reasons people flock to the park.

In 2022, a press release announced that the Welcome Center in Cherryblossomland would be replaced with a new, grander and more accessible structure designed to better accommodate community events. The message came with a reassurance that the bocce courts would be "repositioned" but safe—a nod, no doubt, to the throngs of men who hang out at the courts and play bocce, seemingly nonstop, for hours at a time.

A wide range of activities is available at Weequahic Park as well. It boasts an eighteen-hole golf course—the oldest public course in New Jersey—as well as picnic grounds, athletic fields, playgrounds and a two-mile rubberized track around the lake.

In 2019, the park installed a state-of-the-art field for the Rutgers Scarlet Raiders. The university baseball team holds its home contests on the site, which is made with temperature-controlled material, reducing the likelihood of cancellations due to inclement weather. What today's visitors to Weequahic Park will *not* find is the half-mile track where horse races spanned the nineteenth and twentieth centuries or the grandstands where thousands of spectators looked on.

Although the exact date is in dispute, in the mid-1800s, an agricultural fair and what Charles Cummings, the late Newark historian, described as "more elaborate racing events" came into being. The area became known as the Waverly Fairgrounds, and harness racing was introduced, with the fair taking place from 1857 to 1898. Races were scheduled every weekend from Memorial Day through Columbus Day for more than forty years.

In 1872, Cummings wrote, President Ulysses S. Grant, in town to attend Newark's Industrial Exhibition, was among the spectators. Even as the city had rapidly grown into a highly industrialized center, the grounds on which Weequahic Park now stands and much of the surrounding area remained farmland.

In 1897, the fairgrounds—long a money-losing proposition—were sold to the fledgling Essex County Park Commission. The commission turned to the Olmsteds to develop Weequahic Park. Throughout the design process, harness racing continued unabated, although it then operated under the auspices of the New Jersey Road and Horse Association.

Weequahic's trotters were no small potatoes. The best horses and riders competed on its racetrack for years. In October 1927, the *New York Times* reported that a crowd of forty thousand watched as a new world record was set.

Racing continued without interruption until 1943, when the military intervened and the racetrack was turned into a field hospital for American

The trotters at Weequahic Park. *Courtesy of the Essex County Department of Parks, Recreation, and Cultural Affairs.*

troops. Both the track and the grandstand were partially destroyed over the next couple of years, and it seemed to many that harness racing at Weequahic Park had at last come to an end. And yet, improbably, the area was rehabilitated after the war and, in 1955, horse racing resumed. For the next few years—until the early '60s—it continued, albeit on a more limited basis, under the direction of the Weequahic Park Amateur Trotting Club.

With the trotters now led by amateurs, the *New York Times* reported at the time, harness racing was no longer a millionaire's sport. Instead, the *Times* asserted, it could be enjoyed by those of relatively modest means. A racehorse could be purchased for about $1,000. And maintenance of the animal, depending on the amount of care the owner was willing to take on himself, was available for $75 to $150 a month. It's worth noting that, when adjusted for inflation, that same racehorse would cost more than $10,600 today.

Whatever the monetary value to their owners, Weequahic's racehorses provided pocket change for kids who lived nearby. In an article on the Old

Newark website, one man recalled the money he earned at the tender age of nine. "I 'hot walked' the horses" boarded in the park, he wrote, and cleaned out their stalls, earning two dollars per chore.

That opportunity ended in 1961, when the Essex County Park Commission decided it was time to put the track and field to other uses. The grandstand, which had required considerable repair after being used by the military in the 1940s, stood for several more decades and was ultimately torn down.

PART IV

IDEOLOGY AND ACTIVISM

10

GOING UNDERGROUND

Shortly after the Revolutionary War ended in 1783, many northern states passed laws to abolish slavery. New Jersey was not among them. The state finally passed antislavery legislation in 1804. But, as the very name of the new law reveals, it fell far short of ending slavery.

The Act for the Gradual Abolition of Slavery did nothing for New Jersey residents who were already enslaved. Freedom was years away as well for the children of enslaved women. Female offspring would not be free until they turned twenty-one; males would remain enslaved for an additional four years, until their twenty-fifth birthday.

As the last of the northern states to fully abolish the institution of slavery, New Jersey acquired the unsavory title "Slave State of the North." Slavery's death knell came on January 23, 1866, when Marcus L. Ward, New Jersey's newly installed governor, eliminated it, thereby freeing the last sixteen state residents to be enslaved. It came three years after the Emancipation Proclamation and more than half a year after June 19, 1865—commemorated as Juneteenth, the day on which Texas became the last of the Confederate states to officially end slavery.

For the City of Newark, Juneteenth 2022 proved to be a momentous occasion. That's the day Mayor Ras Baraka officially changed the name of Washington Park to Harriet Tubman Square. A statue of Christopher Columbus that once had a prominent place in the triangular park that borders Washington and Broad Streets in downtown Newark had been removed two years earlier. And soon, Baraka told the crowd on Juneteenth, a monument to the famous abolitionist would replace it.

June 19, 2022, also coincided with the news that the National Park Service had added a Newark site to its extensive Underground Railroad Network. Designed to honor, preserve and promote the history of resistance to enslavement through escape and flight, the NPS's Network to Freedom includes some seven hundred locales in thirty-nine states; Washington, D.C.; and the U.S. Virgin Islands.

Given New Jersey's lengthy delay in putting an end to slavery and the fact that the state was not a hospitable place for people desperately seeking freedom, it is not surprising that some details about Newark's place on the Underground Railroad (UGRR) remain hazy. While free Black Newarkers, some of whom worked as carriage drivers, were involved in the creation of a local way station for fugitives from slavery, the city overall was not a welcoming place for a layover.

That did not prevent abolitionist activity, of course, in either the city or the state. Harriet Tubman worked for a time in Cape May. The seaside town was just across Delaware Bay from Maryland's Eastern Shore, where she had been enslaved. From this vantage point, Tubman embarked on at least thirteen missions leading people from slavery to freedom, setting off on another journey every time she had amassed enough money to lead the way. And legend has it, on a number of occasions Tubman and those she helped ferry to safety headed north by way of Newark.

That, however, appears to be just that—a legend. James Amemasor, PhD, a researcher at the New Jersey Historical Society in Newark who has carefully studied the city's abolitionist activity, said no evidence has been found that Tubman actually came through Newark.

"I do not see how Harriet Tubman would have risked coming here," Amemasor said, noting that the city would not have been a safe place. While some Newarkers were actively engaged in helping those fleeing enslavement, many residents were in favor of slavery. That was at least in part because the city's industrial base relied on cheap southern goods, which were available at low prices only because unpaid laborers produced them.

Amemasor, who served on the committee screening proposed designs for the new Tubman monument, nonetheless enthusiastically supported the decision to honor her. Tubman's work, he pointed out, was no different from what other Blacks were doing in Newark. What she stood for is exactly what Harriet Tubman Square and the monument represent, Amemasor asserted: "The ideals of freedom that our country stands for and that should not be determined by geography."

Built by individuals whose descendents were enslaved, the house at 70 Warren Street was a stop on the Underground Railroad. *New Jersey Historical Society.*

Legend has it, too, that a warren of passageways in the basement of First Presbyterian Church on Broad Street—known to many simply as Old First—was used to ferry fugitives to safety. That, too, lacks evidence to support it. While the congregation was antislavery, Amemasor noted, that does not mean the church was a stop on the Underground Railroad or that its members were integrationists. Many advocated sending people of African descent back to the continent instead.

Evidence does show that a modest house at 70 Warren Street functioned as Newark's Underground Railroad station, along with the Presbyterian Plane Street Colored Church next door. Nicole Lorraine Williams, director of the African-American History Program of the New Jersey Historical Commission, lobbied the NPS for the site's inclusion on its Network to Freedom. On the application to the NPS, Williams described the church and surrounding area as "the nucleus of Black anti-slavery and UGRR education work from Newark."

Neither the house, which was built by people whose ancestors were enslaved, nor the church remains. The land on which they stood is part of a Rutgers University athletic field. Named Frederick Douglass Field, it honors the esteemed activist and abolitionist who spoke at the Plane Street Church in 1849.

Much of what is known about the house on Warren Street and its owner, Jacob D. King, was discovered by Teresa Vega, a cultural anthropologist and genealogist and distant relative of King's. When Vega found that King's home had functioned as a stop on the Underground Railroad, she and another relative embarked on a historic journey. Together, they combed through anything they could find—probate, census and church records and old newspapers, among other documentation. Vega has detailed their findings on the *RadiantRoots* blog (radiantrootsboricuabranches.com).

Jacob King, Vega's third great-uncle by marriage, purchased the tract of land at 70 Warren Street in 1829 for $100. He built the house with the help of family members, some of whom were carpenters, a year later. He apparently planned from the start to use the building as a stopover for individuals fleeing slavery. Old photos, discovered in recent years, reveal removable floorboards, a hidden closet in the cellar, a small escape hatch to the outside and an old Dutch oven believed to have been used to prepare meals for fugitives.

One of eight children, Jacob King was born on April 6, 1806. His father, Dublin King, was Scots-Irish. His mother, Lucy, was formerly enslaved by Abraham Ogden, whose family was among Newark's earliest settlers.

Indeed, a man by the name of Josiah Ogden was at the heart of a break from the church established by Newark's Puritan settlers and a founder of Trinity, the city's first Episcopal church.

In 1829, Jacob King married Mary Thompson in a ceremony at First Presbyterian Church, where the Thompsons were members. Mary's father, Thomas Thompson—also a distant relative of Vega's—had been enslaved by Hercules Daniel Bize, a man of considerable wealth. Upon Bize's death in 1800, Thompson was granted his freedom, as well as property and a stagecoach. In less than ten years, Vega wrote, Thompson had a thriving stagecoach business and became "Newark's richest Free Person of Color."

Jacob and Mary's last surviving child, Ellen C. King, lived for most of her life at the house on 70 Warren Street. She passed away in in 1936 at the age of ninety-seven. But the King family, Vega found, had centuries-old roots in Newark.

A 1912 article in *New York Age* referred to Harriet Brown, a daughter of Jacob King, as "a descendent of one of the oldest colored families in Newark." The article further stated that Brown's forebears settled in the city "150 years ago"—that would have been in the mid to late eighteenth century. But additional research revealed that the family history in the greater Newark area goes back more than four hundred years.

The extended Thompson-King family members "were among the original foot soldiers of freedom who institutionalized what became known as the Underground Railroad in the Northeast," Vega declared at *Activate! The Legacy of Frederick Douglass and Abolition in Newark* in 2019. "Our ancestors are descended from the Ramapough Lenape," who have lived in the tristate area for millennia, Vega added, as well as "one of the first 'Spanish Negroes,' enslaved people from all over West Africa, the first enslaved people from Madagascar, and European (Dutch, Scots-Irish, British, and French Huguenot) colonizers."

Although neither Thomas Thompson nor his home is as widely known as the King home at 70 Warren Street, it played a key role in helping those fleeing slavery. Fugitives would leave King's home via the escape hatch—a crawl space of sorts—in the basement and make their way through the woods to the Thompson property a short distance away. From there, they could resume their journey, hidden away in a stagecoach.

Two students at Rutgers University–Newark created a video, *Simulation of the Underground Railroad in Newark*, and posted it on Vimeo (vimeo. com/244849361). Viewers get a bird's-eye view of the likely layout of 70 Warren Street, with particular detail of the various elements embedded in the cellar. They can also see the wooded area that those seeking freedom would have traversed to reach the Thompson house and barn nearby. There, they would be hidden in a carriage and ferried away.

It is this work—and, indeed, the work of freed Blacks and others not only from Newark but also in many other states along the way—that the new Harriet Tubman monument celebrates. Called *Shadow of a Face* and officially unveiled on March 9, 2023, it was created to give Newarkers a greater understanding of the institution of slavery and the struggle of people of color to be free. "It is a part of this continuous history," said Nina Cooke John, the architect-artist who designed the two-and-a-half-story monument.

In highlighting the renaming of the park and the replacement of the Columbus statue, Mayor Ras Baraka stated, "We thought it wasn't enough to remove statues. We thought we should be replacing them and talking about the history itself. And so Harriet Tubman obviously came to mind for us because the Underground Railroad actually existed in Newark in that downtown community." The focus on Tubman is part of his administration's ongoing effort to reconsider "who sits on pedestals in this mostly black and brown city," Baraka said.

And yet, despite the sheer size of the new monument, Cooke John's design does not place Tubman on a pedestal. Instead, it invites visitors to walk inside and "feel as if they are part of her," she said. Because those escaping slavery relied on the North Star to guide them—and Tubman herself saw its presence as a sign from God—the monument features a series of intertwined profiles of Tubman, all connecting with a North Star, lit at night, at her head.

Other features include a circular outer wall with a timeline of the life of Tubman, who risked her life not only leading enslaved people to freedom but also as a spy for the Union during the Civil War. Relevant aspects of the area's history—featuring information about New Jersey Safe Houses, for instance, and Black Soldiers in the Revolutionary War—are written on an inner wall. On the outside, an oversized image of Tubman's face sits at eye level, a feature Cooke John described as a deliberate attempt to encourage visitors to "look into her eyes and touch her face and connect to her, to her humanity." Tiles designed by community members attending a workshop at the Newark Museum of Art are embedded in the monument as well. "The tiles represent the people of Newark and your struggles, your own liberation stories integrated with the liberation stories of Harriet Tubman," Cooke John said.

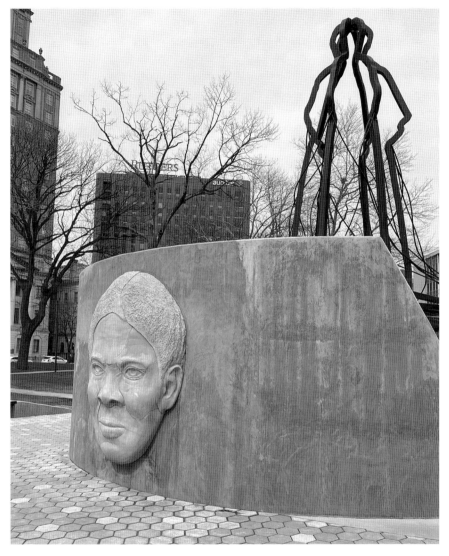

Shadow of a Face, a multifaceted, two-and-a-half-story Harriet Tubman monument, was dedicated in 2023. *Helen Lippman.*

Hearing is as important as vision and touch to the overall experience of *Shadow of a Face.* Voices of community members—captured in sound booths at the Newark Library with the help of Audible (both of which are across from Harriet Tubman Square) are heard on broadcasts around the monument. Queen Latifah, a Newark native, is part of the multimedia experience. She can be heard telling Tubman's life story.

11

FIGHTING FOR WOMEN'S SUFFRAGE

O verall, Newark was not a leader in the battle for women's right to vote. But by a twist of fate, the city took center stage on February 12, 1913, when a small but dedicated procession of suffragists and their supporters began the first leg of a journey that would culminate in the nation's first major political protest march in Washington, D.C.

While momentum in support of the vote for women had expanded in New Jersey and elsewhere since the turn of the century, opposition, especially in Newark, remained strong. In a talk on "Women's Suffrage in Newark," sponsored by the Newark History Society to mark the centennial of the constitutional amendment that guaranteed women's right to vote, historian and Rutgers professor George Robb stated, "Newark was at the center of the anti-suffrage movement in New Jersey." In 1912, the National Association Opposed to Women's Suffrage (NAOWS) was founded. Shortly thereafter, a New Jersey chapter headquartered in a building on Broad Street in Newark sprang up.

Perhaps the clearest evidence that suffragists still faced a long, uphill slog in New Jersey dates from 1915, when a state referendum on women's right to vote appeared on the ballot. The measure was defeated by a higher margin in Newark than anywhere else in the state.

Much of the opposition to women's suffrage in this highly industrialized city was led by well-to-do women. Most were white, native-born Protestants, and many were married to prominent businessmen. The business community feared that if women had the vote, they would institute stringent regulatory measures likely to erode corporate profit.

The looming threat of Prohibition—a sobering prospect in a city that had some 1,400 saloons and where breweries ranked as one of the leading industries—was also a key concern. Anti-suffragists so feared restrictions on alcoholic beverages that they launched an ad campaign proclaiming, "A Vote for Women's Suffrage Is a Vote for Prohibition."

Many worried, too, that if women gained the right to vote, they would outlaw child labor, another move that the business community perceived as a threat to their profits. More broadly, anti-suffragists thought that allowing women to vote would propel wives and mothers out of the home and into the political arena. This was highlighted in a cartoon in a local newspaper picturing a frazzled-looking dad and his young children, ominously captioned, "Where is our wandering Mama tonight?"

Despite the opposition, the suffrage movement did gain some strength in Newark as in the rest of the state. By 1912, an article had appeared in *Rutgers Library Journal* stating that New Jersey Woman Suffrage Association had "evolved into a modern political pressure group." On October 12 of that year, the state had its first suffrage parade—in Newark. The event attracted some eight hundred to one thousand women and men representing suffragist coalitions throughout New Jersey.

Still, despite having begun as part of the American women's movement officially kicked off at the Seneca Falls Convention in 1848 in New York, the struggle for women suffrage had little to show. Sixty-four years later, women had the right to vote in just four states: Colorado, Idaho, Utah and Wyoming. Yet rather than push for a national amendment, organizers had opted to continue to pursue a state-by-state strategy that was painfully slow and largely ineffective.

That's the climate in which two prominent American suffragists—Alice Paul and Lucy Burns, both of whom had joined the far more raucous battle for women's vote in England—found themselves when they returned to the United States in 1912. To Paul, especially, it seemed obvious that a national amendment was the only way to go. Yet during Woodrow Wilson's campaign to win the nomination for the presidency and, later, as president-elect before being sworn in on March 4, 1913, he made it clear that he had no intention of taking up the cause.

"For the purposes of the 1912 campaign," Rebecca Boggs Roberts wrote in *Suffragists in Washington, D.C.*, Wilson "cloaked his misogynist views in the mantle of states' rights." When confronted by a suffragist at a campaign event, he responded, "Women suffrage, madam, is not a question that is dealt with by the National Government at all. I am here only as a representative of the national party."

To change the narrative and get the attention of Wilson and the country, Paul sought permission from the National American Woman Suffrage Association (NAWSA) to hold a march in the capital around the time of his inauguration. She also planned to deliver a letter to the incoming president. The letter, which would urge Wilson to ensure that women's suffrage would become a reality during his presidency and warn him that the nation's women would be watching his administration more closely than they had scrutinized that of any of his predecessors, does not appear to have ever been delivered. Instead, a delegation met with Wilson less than two weeks after the inauguration. In response to the women's impassioned plea, Wilson was less than forthcoming. He hadn't thought much about the matter, he told the delegation, but promised to give it "my most careful consideration."

NAWSA agreed to Paul's request after she pledged to raise the money for the groundbreaking event. She began planning for the parade by seeking two concessions she deemed vital to its success: a permit to hold the suffragist march on March 3, just one day before Wilson's inauguration; and a guarantee that the suffragists be allowed to march along Pennsylvania Avenue for more than a mile.

The date was secured without difficulty; permission to use the Pennsylvania Avenue parade route was not. The District of Columbia's chief of police balked, fearing that the security needed to manage such a large undertaking just a day before the presidential inauguration would be too daunting a task. Paul, however, refused to budge. She went over his head, directly contacting the city commissioner who oversaw the Capitol Police and taking her case to the media. Her campaign took time and energy, but eventually the chief of police relented.

With that set, plans for the small group of suffragists who intended to hike from Manhattan to Washington, D.C., began to take shape. There would be fifteen marchers, plus their leader, Rosalie "the General" Jones. Their trek would begin with a kickoff event in New York City on February 12.

The rally, detailed in a *Ms.* magazine article published a century later, attracted a largely sympathetic crowd. Among the attendees were about two hundred women and men who pledged to join the procession for the first leg of their journey. That, however, is when fate intervened, giving Newark the opportunity to make its mark in the annals of suffragist history.

The marchers had barely set off when they encountered roads that were impassable, forcing an abrupt change of plans. Newark, easily reachable by train from Manhattan, became the new point of embarkation. Ida ("the Colonel") Craft, an event organizer and a lead hiker, was so upset by this turn of events that "she spent some of her time on board marching back and forth from one end of the train to the other," David Dismore, archivist for the Feminist Majority Foundation, wrote in *Ms*. "Her opening and closing of doors irritated the passengers and conductors," he noted, "but it did succeed in at least partly fulfilling Craft's desire to walk from New York City to Washington, D.C."

When they disembarked from the Hudson Tube Train in Newark and began forming a procession, the sixteen suffragists who had vowed to hike all the way to Washington, D.C., slowly inched their way along Broad Street. Their numbers swelled as supporters, including some members of the Newark Equal Suffrage League and the Essex County Suffrage Society, followed. Clad in hats and heavy overcoats to withstand the wintry weather, the marchers were an impressive sight.

Those at the head of the procession likely had momentary pangs of fear, Dismore wrote, when a lineup of mounted police headed toward them. If

Suffragist marchers began their historic hike to Washington, D.C., in Newark. *Library of Congress.*

so, their dismay would have dissipated as soon as they spotted the yellow "Votes for Women" pennant "fluttering from the saddle" of the lieutenant in charge.

In the more than two weeks it took the marchers to reach the District of Columbia, their numbers ebbed and flowed. Some supporters walked with the group for part of the journey and then departed, while others joined in at various junctures. Although the trek generated much positive publicity, the marchers also encountered opposition and considerable hostility at times. But that paled in comparison to what they faced in the nation's capital.

The parade itself was carefully choreographed. Women on horseback led the way, followed by a wagon with a huge sign. Referred to as the "Great Demand Banner," it boldly called for an amendment to the U.S. Constitution enfranchising women. Floats represented each of the countries in which women had the vote—Australia, Finland, New Zealand and Norway. Then came affinity groups, sorted by profession, state delegation or alma mater. Marching bands, golden chariots and a huge reproduction of the Liberty Bell rounded out the procession, which was stalled from the start.

The 1913 Woman's Suffrage Parade, held the day before Woodrow Wilson's presidential inauguration, was carefully choreographed. *Library of Congress.*

Spectators crowded into the roadway, Roberts wrote, making it impossible for the marchers to proceed. The promised police protection and escort did not materialize, and the agreed-on route was not cleared. One of the women on horseback charged with kicking off the parade later described what she could see on Pennsylvania Avenue as a "horrible, howling mob." And, Roberts reported, Paul herself saw Boy Scouts "valiantly holding the crowd back in places, while the policemen did nothing."

Finally, with the crowd swelled to hundreds of thousands, D.C. officials called in the cavalry. "Their horses were driven into the throngs and whirled and wheeled until hooting men and women were forced to retreat," the *Washington Post* wrote.

In the meantime, Wilson and his entourage arrived in D.C. via train to prepare for the next day's inauguration. There they were met by a modest crowd, Roberts wrote. When Wilson asked where all the people were, the police responded, "Watching the suffrage parade."

All was not well with those marching in the parade, however. Ambulances came and went for hours. At least one hundred people were taken to local hospitals. Many more escaped serious injury but were nonetheless battered, furious and freezing. Yet Alice Paul—still clad in the academic robe she had planned to wear for the duration of the march—took a good look around. "And then she smiled," Roberts reported. "It was perfect."

Paul's instinct was spot-on. As she suspected, witnessing the chaos and near riot that the marchers endured convinced many otherwise skeptical reporters to support the suffrage cause. Roberts cited the words of Ohio congressman Clyde Tavenner, who dramatically described the effect of what transpired: "More votes were made for women suffrage in the city of Washington on the afternoon of March 3rd than will perhaps ever be made in the same length of time so long as the government stands."

One problem that had long confronted the suffrage movement involved the often competing needs and goals of different constituencies. "Suffragists included women who were rich and poor, Black and white, native-born and immigrants, sometimes in alliance and sometimes in conflict." So stated Noelle Lorraine Williams, director of the African-American History Program at the New Jersey Historical Commission, in a presentation at the Newark Public Library now available on YouTube.

One sticking point was race. The National Association of Colored Women and leaders of other African American women's groups had long maintained that voting rights for Black women were inseparable from the problem of Black men's disenfranchisement. The stance of the predominantly white women who dominated the national suffragist movement was that their quest centered on gender, not race. And in the lead-up to the March 3 protest march, issues of race took center stage.

Paul, a Quaker, apparently wanted the historic event to be inclusive, as did NAWSA leadership. But, she was warned, a fully integrated parade would likely cause some white delegations, particularly those from southern states, to withdraw their support and refuse to march.

Paul attempted to have it both ways, keeping the struggle quiet and suggesting that an African American contingency march together near the rear of the parade. That's not exactly what happened. When a group of women from Howard, a historically Black university, wanted to march with the other college groups, they were given the okay but kept off of the official program.

Other Black suffragists refused to be segregated and ended up marching without hindrance. The journalist Ida B. Wells, a founder of the Alpha Suffrage Club for Black women, simply stood along the sidelines until the marchers representing Illinois reached her, and then she took her place with her state delegation. Mary Church Terrell, who in 1896 became the first president of the National Association of Colored Women, "defiantly marched throughout the parade," Alison M. Parker, author of *Unceasing Militant: The Life of Mary Church Terrell*, wrote.

Despite the momentum that resulted from the parade and its attendant publicity, Woodrow Wilson's support for women's suffrage was still several years away. In May 1919, the House of Representatives passed the Nineteenth Amendment, granting women the right to vote; the Senate followed two weeks later. In 1920, New Jersey became the twenty-ninth state to ratify the amendment. And on August 24, 1920, Tennessee became the thirty-sixth state to do so, thereby reaching the three-fourths threshold needed to ratify the constitutional amendment. After a struggle that lasted more than seventy years, American women finally had the right to vote.

12

CHASING COMMUNISTS

Are you now or have you ever been a member of the Communist Party? Although the wording differed from case to case, that was the key question put to everyone summoned to testify before the House Un-American Activities Committee (HUAC). Created in 1938 and lasting until the mid-'70s, HUAC was hailed by some for cracking down on Communists and castigated by others for running roughshod over Americans' constitutional rights.

All told, HUAC interrogators questioned some three thousand people, including more than thirty men and women here in Newark. In the spring and summer of 1955, people from all walks of life—teachers, doctors, social workers, World War II veterans and, especially, current or former union organizers—were summoned to the city's Federal Building to testify. Their words, along with those of their interrogators, have been memorialized in two bound volumes by a British publisher, Forgotten Books.

By the time of the Newark hearings, there had been Communists in the city for more than twenty-five years. The American Communist Party, initially known as the Workers' Party, was established in 1919, following a split in the Socialist Party of America after the Bolshevik Revolution. The party rapidly organized in cities nationwide.

The first recorded evidence of activity from a Newark branch dates back to the summer of 1919, historian Warren Grover reported in a Newark History Society presentation on the Newark Communist Party. On a Sunday morning in August of that year, residents of the Ironbound section—known at the time as Little Russia—found circulars stuffed under their doors denouncing capitalism and calling for the overthrow of the government.

While the American Communist Party was new at the time, political activism was not. There had long been Newarkers who were affiliated with the Socialist Party and involved in the labor movement. Italian anarchists, Russian Marxists, German socialists and Eastern European Jews affiliated with the Workmen's Circle were all potential members of the newly formed Communist Party as well. The Yiddish-speaking Workmen's Circle supported many Jewish immigrants, and its membership split into Communist and Socialist factions after the division in the Socialist Party.

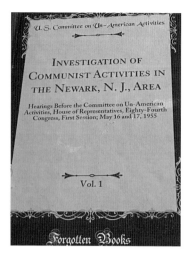

The transcripts of House Un-American Activities Committee hearings in Newark in 1955 are memorialized in two bound volumes. *Helen Lippman.*

The year the American Communist Party was formed, bombs exploded in a number of big cities. The plot was ultimately traced, not to the Communists but to a small group of Italian anarchists. Nonetheless, the hunt for Communists, led since late 1919 by J. Edgar Hoover, was on.

In early 1920, raids and crackdowns—known as the "Palmer Raids" for Attorney General A. Mitchell Palmer—resulted in some five thousand arrests. The *Newark News*, a leading city paper, ran an editorial debunking the threat of "the Red Scare," Grover reported. Two months later, when Newark police raided a dance at which none of the radicals they had arrest warrants for were found, the newspaper asked whether "any form of propaganda against the United States [could] be worse than these very acts of lawlessness perpetrated in its name."

In addition to the raids, police and city officials routinely refused to permit groups associated with the Communist Party to speak or to assemble. William J. Brennan, father of the late Supreme Court justice, served as Newark Commissioner and Public Safety Director and steadfastly refused to sign off on a joint rally of the American Civil Liberties Union and the International Labor Defense (ILD). Brennan, Grover reported, told a leader of the ILD, "You can't talk in Newark…not while we run this town."

Despite the opposition, the party's presence in Newark grew. The Young Communist League, an offshoot designed to attract younger, often second-generation Americans, formed a Newark branch in 1923. That same year, the party's official newspaper, the *Daily Worker*, established an office in Newark.

In the 1930s, Ellen Schrecker wrote in *The Age of McCarthyism*, the Depression and the rise of fascism in Europe transformed the American Communist Party from a "tiny, faction-ridden sect composed primarily of radical immigrants into the most important and dynamic organization on the left." Over the course of the decade, she added, party membership soared, going from some 7,500 to about 55,000. "Communists organized demonstrations of the unemployed in Chicago, protected young African Americans against lynching in Alabama, and led strikes of California farmworkers," Schrecker observed.

Party members with experience as labor organizers were particularly in demand. By the end of World War II, she wrote, about a fifth of unions affiliated with the Congress of Industrial Organizations (CIO) were "within the Communist party orbit." In the Newark area, building and supporting labor unions and fighting against abysmal working conditions became a major focus of many Communists.

Although members of the Communist Party had long been targeted by regional and national governments, the start of the Cold War shortly after the war's end intensified anti-Communist coalitions and activities. Thus, the climate was right for McCarthyism to thrive. Anti-Communist sentiment, Schrecker wrote, was exploited by special-interest groups. By far the most important of these "were those segments of the business community who opposed organized labor."

With anti-Communist activity reaching a fever pitch, some ten thousand Americans lost their jobs, sometimes because of actual participation in the party. In other cases, people had alleged affiliations with Communist-linked associations. At times, people who were subpoenaed by HUAC were fired immediately. Others, as in the case of three Newark teachers who were interrogated at the hearings, lost their jobs after pleading the Fifth Amendment. Newark-based academics, both at Rutgers and the Newark College of Engineering, were fired as well.

Many more, primarily those in the entertainment industry, were put on the notorious blacklist. As Mark Goodson, a prominent TV producer, later testified, "There were no differentiations made between Communists, Communist sympathizers, those who had lunch with Communist sympathizers, those who knew somebody who had lunch with Communist sympathizers, and so forth." Goodson added, "In certain cases it even—I'm ashamed to say—included the elimination of people from shows because they had the same name as members of the Communist Party."

Early in the 1940s, the government began keeping a list of "subversive" organizations, and in 1947, the first attorney general's list was released. On it were not only the American Communist Party but also numerous groups thought to be "Communist fronts," as well as the Ku Klux Klan and the Nazi Party. In November 1950, the list—officially named the Attorney General's List of Totalitarian, Fascist, Communist, Subversive, and Other Organizations—cited 197 organizations, some with benign-sounding names, like the American Lincoln Brigade, the League of American Writers and the Washington Bookshop Organization. It later grew to include nearly 300 groups. Millions of workers had their affiliations scrutinized or were required to sign loyalty oaths, which often included not only swearing that they were loyal to the U.S. government but also disavowing membership in any organization on the subversives' list.

In 1955, within a month of the first HUAC hearings in Newark, the city ordered its seven thousand employees to sign loyalty oaths and fill out questionnaires about both past and present affiliations. Ironically, though, the Newark City Council did an abrupt about-face, rescinding the requirement almost the moment it was issued. It was tabled, according to the *New York Times*, because the individual who had initiated the order did not want to subject staffers to so broad an interrogation. As Schrecker observed, most of the groups on the list did have some link to Communist activity. On the other hand, some individuals who interacted with the organizations remained unaware of such ties and were neither Communists nor Communist supporters.

That was not true of those who were interrogated by HUAC, most of whom either had been or were still connected in some way with the party. A couple of former members, who had apparently agreed to testify about the work they had been engaged in and to "name names," were praised as patriots. One such witness was congratulated for "coming to the point where you place your country ahead of the damnable Communist conspiracy."

In many more cases, though, the hearings were circular, yielding few acknowledgements of activity that could be incriminating. Witnesses repeatedly invoked the Fifth Amendment, refusing to answer questions about alleged involvement in the party. Often, the interrogators repeated the same query, with slightly different wording, again and again—and got the same response.

At times, the exchanges were almost comical. One witness, a physician charged with heading a "doctors' cell of the Communist Party in Newark," declined to say whether he was a party member, "on the grounds that the very existence of this committee is a violation of the fundamental doctrine of separation of powers upon which our democracy is based." After insisting that there be only one question on the floor at a time—and being assured that all other questions were withdrawn—he cited the First Amendment to the Constitution as a reason for refusing to answer. As he began ticking off the freedoms the First Amendment guaranteed, he was abruptly stopped with this admonishment: "Just say the first amendment. We know what it contains. We are lawyers and you are a doctor. Give us reasons."

In response, the doctor cited not only the First and Fifth Amendments, but also the Sixth, Eighth, Ninth and Tenth. Unable to pierce this armor, his interrogator ultimately declared that he had no further questions.

Another witness, after a series of similar responses, noted that others who came before HUAC had been asked what proposals they could offer to do away with subversion in the country. "I would like to be asked that question," the witness told his interrogators. They replied that he would not, because he had accused the U.S. government of being a tyranny.

"I love this Government and the American people," the witness insisted.

"You love it enough to call it a tyranny," his interrogator responded.

After a couple of similar exchanges, the HUAC representative concluded, "I am ashamed of you....You are excused."

HUAC's demise occurred not long after the committee began investigating those who opposed the Vietnam War. In the late '60s, investigations of noted antiwar activists Abbie Hoffman and Jerry Rubin—"both of whom attended the hearings at various times wearing a Santa Claus or a Revolutionary War patriot outfit," according to The First Amendment Encyclopedia— "contributed to the rising unpopularity of HUAC." In 1969, its name was changed to the Internal Security Committee, and in 1975, it was abolished.

13

NEWARK TO NAZIS: GET OUT

Talk of a riot in Newark invariably focuses on July 1967, when racial inequities and the beating of a Black taxi driver by white police officers triggered a multi-day uprising that ended in death and destruction. Few are even aware of another riot—the so-called victory on Springfield Avenue—that predated the '67 rebellion by thirty-four years.

There are far more significant differences between these two momentous events than the three-plus decades that separate them. Most important, the 1933 brawl—labeled a "riot" by city police and some historians but characterized as a "near riot" by the *New York Times*—had a positive effect on the city. It was an epic battle between Nazi supporters—a growing movement in America after Hitler took power in Germany and in the years leading up to World War II—and militant anti-Nazis right here in Newark.

Another key difference: The 1967 uprising lasted for five days; the anti-Nazi riot occurred on October 16, 1933, and was over in a single night.

Hitler's ascendency to chancellor of Germany in January 1933 fueled a surge of Nazi supporters abroad. The first such group to form in the United States adopted the seemingly innocuous name Friends of the New Germany. The organization flourished in New York. But in order to gain the sought-after influence in New Jersey governmental affairs, the Friends needed a presence in the state's largest and most highly industrialized city.

Evidence of Nazis in Newark soon surfaced. Notices adorned with swastikas appeared on trees and telephone poles; men clad in the Brownshirt uniforms worn by members of the Nazi Party in Germany were spotted on occasion; and, as early as April 1933, rumors that the Friends were

A symbol of the German American Bund, so named after Friends of the New Germany were accused of being unpatriotic. *Wikipedia*.

planning a gathering in Newark quickly spread. The presence of Nazi supporters struck fear in residents of the old neighborhood, where for years Jews and Germans had lived peaceably. Older Jews, many of whom vividly recalled fleeing poverty, prejudice and pogroms in eastern Europe, became particularly upset.

The Friends held their first meeting in Newark at a German American event space on Springfield Avenue not far from the Irvington border. The name of the facility: Schwabenhalle.

The initial gathering was small, but it was a precursor of things to come. About a month later, the Friends scheduled an event at a hall in nearby Irvington. This time, four hundred people attended. A clash broke out but was quickly quashed by police with tear gas and riot gear.

The combative anti-Nazis in that case were members of the Newark chapter of the American Communist Party, which had formed in 1932. But soon another group emerged to take the lead in fighting Nazis, organized at the behest of a prominent Jewish gangster named Abner Zwillman.

Popularly known as Longie—a likely reference to his height—Zwillman, at six feet, two inches tall, towered over the vast majority of his contemporaries. He was "Newark's undisputed crime boss," Warren Grover, author of *Nazis in Newark*, wrote, as well as "one of the most powerful crime bosses in the country."

Longie, whom the press often referred to as New Jersey's Al Capone, was "a leading bootlegger during Prohibition who was active in labor racketeering and gambling enterprises." He recruited Nat Arno (née Sidney Nathaniel Abramowitz), a prizefighter with well over one hundred bouts under his belt, to organize a gang of Nazi fighters. Arno, a longtime accomplice of Longie, compiled a motley crew of ex-boxers, thugs and criminals, most but not all of whom were Jewish. They became known as the Minutemen.

The name harkened back to the armed militia ready to respond at a moment's notice during the Revolutionary War. Newark's Minutemen had the same mission more than 150 years later. So, when the Friends announced their next meeting in Newark, scheduled in late September to celebrate the birthday of Paul von Hindenburg, who had led the German army in World War I, the Minutemen did not hesitate.

In preparation for the event, they shrouded iron pipes in newspapers and stashed them in an alleyway near Schwabenhalle. Then they waited and struck when the event was underway. The Minutemen tossed rocks and stink bombs through the windows into the hall and began beating anyone they found wearing a Nazi uniform. And then, as quickly as they had begun, the Nazi fighters fled, leaving a few attendees with injuries but ensuring that all the attackers were long gone by the time the police arrived.

No arrests resulted from the events that occurred that night, but there was an effect that the Friends strongly objected to: Congress announced an investigation of Nazi activities in the United States. The Friends responded by planning a huge protest rally, to be held at Schwabenhalle. They vowed to have their own security forces on hand. Newark police pledged sufficient deployment to avoid a repeat of the battle.

The upcoming rally was awash in publicity, with coverage by both the media and the organizers themselves. It was billed as the Friends' biggest rally to date, setting the stage, Grover wrote, "for Newark to be the first major American battleground in the struggle against domestic Nazism."

On the evening of October 16, 1933, more than eight hundred Nazi supporters arrived, quickly filling the seats in the banquet hall and leaving standing room only. Undetected among those squeezing into the meeting space, according to Grover, were some fifty Minutemen.

Crowds amassed outside as well. About one thousand people had gathered, the *Times* reported the next day; Grover's count was far higher. By 10:00 p.m., he wrote, "2,000 people clogged the area around Schwabenhalle."

Springfield Avenue was jam-packed "with sightseers driving up and down the street," Grover added. "The air was filled with the sound of police sirens, as squad cars fighting the traffic tried to get to the scene. Over 200 police were there now," with officers, some on motorcycles, others brandishing nightsticks and anticipating reinforcement from seven precincts, at the ready. On the podium inside the hall stood an oversized banner of a swastika, flanked with a German flag on one side and an American flag on the other.

The Minutemen waited as the president of the Friends spoke, then prepared to depart as another speaker took the stage. As he began railing against Jews for "bringing disorder to Germany," Arno made his move. He and his cohorts threw rocks and stink bombs into the meeting hall. Pandemonium ensued, prompting panicky shouts for help. Recognizing that no more speeches would take place, the police began ushering people out. And the Nazi fighters pounced.

The fighting went on and on, reportedly extending for twelve blocks and continuing well past midnight. Nazi supporters are thought to have incurred most of the injuries, but most fled without seeking medical help. Just three people were hospitalized, and seven—five of whom were anti-Nazi fighters—were arrested.

From 1933 to 1940, when Arno was drafted into the army, he was at the helm of the Minutemen. But, Grover pointed out, much of Arno's strength and success "derived from the fact that public officials, the police, and the press knew that he was Longie Zwillman's man." Zwillman paid the bills, provided jobs and garnered insider information about the plans of the Nazi supporters, and his influence was a key factor in the Minutemen's mostly lenient treatment. While the struggle against Nazis in the United States—and in Newark in particular—endured as long as the war went on, the victory on Springfield Avenue played a major part in keeping Nazi presence in Newark to a minimum.

14

WOMEN IN THE COCKPIT

O n May 1941, the P-47 Thunderbolt made its maiden flight. The following March—three months after the United States declared war on Japan—the first of the legendary fighter planes was delivered to the military. By 1945, Republic Aviation had produced 15,683 of the aircraft, the majority of them at its facility on Long Island. Before the P-47s saw combat, however, each made its maiden voyage—from Farmingdale, New York, to Newark.

The *P* in the name of the plane stood for "Pursuit," a U.S. Army Air Force designation for fighter planes. It was especially apt in this case, for pursue is what the P-47 did, more effectively, many say, than any other World War II aircraft.

The words used by former military men reminiscing about the P-47 leave little doubt of its might. Those familiar with it have variously described the plane as the toughest fighter ever built; a World War II beast of the airways; unparalleled as a ground-support aircraft and dogfighter; a brick outhouse that could do the dirtiest of the dirty work; and the ruler of the skies.

According to *Smithsonian Magazine*, a fully loaded P-47 "topped out at more than 17,500 pounds." The plane was bulky, nicknamed "the jug," apparently because of its appearance when standing on its nose. Yet despite its weight and shape, the aircraft was exceedingly nimble. By the end of the war, the Thunderbolt had completed more than half a million missions and dropped 132,000 tons of bombs. The fighter plane lived up to its reputation for being virtually indestructible, amassing what *Smithsonian Magazine* labeled "an exceptionally low" loss rate.

It wasn't only the aircraft that was extraordinary, though. Julia Lauria-Blum, a contributing editor for *Metropolitan Airport News*, has shined a light on the pilots—all women—who ferried the P-47s from the Long Island facility where they rolled off the production line to the Atlantic Overseas Air Service Command in Newark. She curated a permanent exhibit at the American Airpower Museum at the old Republic site in Farmingdale that honors the all-female World War II crew known as the Women Airforce Service Pilots (WASP).

Most Americans are familiar with Rosie the Riveter, the iconic figure who symbolized the determination of women who stepped into traditionally male jobs while the men were off fighting in the Second World War. We've all heard stories of the stoic women who labored in factories and shipyards, operated machinery and worked on production lines during the war. Far less well known is that in the early 1940s there was an ample supply of women who were able and eager to do the work previously done by male pilots now serving overseas. Or that from 1942 until the end of 1944, when the WASP program was shut down, the female pilots performed admirably.

Not surprisingly, though, inequities associated with gender were evident from the start. For one, men who wanted to fly for the military could be novices. Not so for women. "The military trained male pilots from scratch," NPR's Susan Stamberg reported, "but not the female civilian volunteers."

It is notable, too, that the female pilots were civilians, unlike their male counterparts. The women were told that they would be admitted to the military, thereby qualifying for higher pay and all the benefits that military status conferred. But that promise failed to materialize, and in 1944, a bill to militarize the female pilots was defeated.

The impetus for the use of female pilots came from two accomplished women. Nancy Harkness Love, a stunt flyer and racer who earned her pilot's license at the age of sixteen, wrote to an officer of the U.S. Air Corps in 1940 suggesting that women be used to ferry planes for the military. At first, she encountered resistance. Within months of the attack on Pearl Harbor, however, Love was charged with establishing a group of female pilots to transport aircraft from factories to seaports and air bases.

Love assembled a team of twenty-eight. All had to meet stringent requirements, most notably that each woman must have accumulated five hundred hours of flying time. The unit, which Love commanded, was designated the Women's Auxiliary Ferrying Squadron (WAFS) and based in Wilmington, Delaware.

Jacqueline Cochran, a world-famous aviator who would go on to become the first woman to break the sound barrier, had a similar idea. By late 1942, she had convinced officers of the air corps that far more women were needed to fly military aircraft nationwide. In November of that year, Cochran founded the Women's Flying Training Detachment in Houston. The requirements for applicants were less stringent than those Love's pilots faced. The recruits needed a minimum of two hundred hours in the air, a requirement that later was pushed back to a mere thirty-five hours.

Some 25,000 women, including many who had learned to fly simply so that they could qualify, answered the call. Of those, only 1,830 were accepted as trainees; 1,074 graduated and were admitted to Cochran's detachment. The following year, Love's and Cochran's groups merged and became the WASP. "They were the crème de la crème," Lauria-Blum says. "Eventually they flew every aircraft in the AAF's arsenal" and engaged in virtually every type of flight except combat missions. The ferrying operations of the WASP logged some sixty million miles.

Transporting P-47s alone was a daunting job. Toward the end of 1944, Lauria-Blum recalled, there could be as many as twenty-eight P-47s a day rolling off Republic Aircraft's production line waiting to be ferried to Newark. The WASP assigned to the Farmingdale plant were based in Wilmington. The pilots would come to Long Island, stay in nearby hotels and line up to ferry the planes to their point of embarkation. It wasn't unusual for the same woman to make multiple trips in a single day, returning to Farmingdale by cargo plane and flying yet another Thunderbolt to the Atlantic Overseas Air Service Command.

Once the planes arrived at the command's Newark headquarters, they were partially disassembled, prepared for shipment and delivered by flatbed to the docks either by transport truck or barge. Cranes lifted them onto aircraft carriers, officially known as aircraft escort vessels, for shipment overseas.

In the rush to keep up with the demand for the Thunderbolts, a pilot often climbed into the cockpit of a new plane and prepared to take off as soon it came off the production line, without any inspection or testing. Accidents, in flight or in training, were inevitable. All told, thirty-eight members of the WASP lost their lives in the line of duty, and many more incurred injuries. Neither the pilots nor their families received any benefits, however, due to their lack of military status.

Not only was a bid to militarize the female pilots defeated, but also by mid-1944, their entire program had come under threat. With the war

Women Airforce Service Pilots flew P-47 fighter planes from Farmingdale, New York, to Newark for shipment overseas. *Courtesy of Julia Lauria-Blum / American Airpower Museum.*

appearing to wind down, training programs for male pilots were halted, and the instructors—terrified of being drafted and desperately needing work—fought for the right to take over the women's jobs. An intensive lobbying effort to shut down the WASP ensued.

Ironically, the anti-WASP campaign coincided with "10 Grand Day"—that is, the day Republic Aviation manufactured the ten thousandth P-47. On September 20, 1944, the women drew straws to determine who would have the honor of ferrying this historic plane. Teresa James, who thought of the Thunderbolt as her baby, picked the short straw.

James, one of the first female pilots and an ace aviator who qualified to fly fifty-four types of civilian and military aircraft, was chosen to ferry the historic plane. From Port Newark, it would embark on its journey to the Italian Front.

Yet this honor clashed with the upcoming demise of the WASP. Just three months later, on December 20, 1944, the program was officially deactivated. But that was not the end of the story.

Ace aviator Teresa James was chosen to ferry the ten thousandth P-47 to Newark. *Courtesy of Julia Lauria-Blum/American Airpower Museum.*

More than thirty years later, according to a segment on PBS Thirteen, "The women pilots of World War II were shocked by a series of headlines in the paper." The U.S. Air Force had announced that women were going to be allowed to serve as military pilots for the first time. "It really set a bomb under all of us" one former WASP recalled. "I thought, 'Come on, after all we put into that program.'"

But this was the 1970s, not the 1940s, and times had changed. In the World War II years, the media reflected the prevailing conviction that women had no legitimate claim to jobs that were rightfully the purview of men. Three decades later, the public was sympathetic to the plight of the "fly girls," particularly to their lack of benefits. One writer reported on a particularly tragic story about a member of the WASP who had died in the line of duty. Not only was her funeral not paid for by the government, but her coworkers also had to pass a hat to raise the money required to send her body home.

In 1976, the women found "a powerful champion" in Senator Barry Goldwater, who had been a World War II pilot himself. They mounted a campaign for public and congressional support, using documentation and testimony showing the many ways they had functioned as a military force.

The following year, they succeeded. In the fall of 1977, both the House and the Senate voted to grant the WASP military status and to make the former pilots eligible for veterans' benefits. For many of the women, PBS reported on *American Experience*, "the victory meant more than financial support from the government. It was an acknowledgment of their service and accomplishments during the war." As one veteran said, "We were finally recognized for what we had done thirty years before." Another added that the measure "gave the families of the girls that were killed a feeling that they died for their country."

But even that wasn't the final chapter. After another three decades had passed, the WASP finally received full recognition. On July 1, 2009, President Barack Obama signed into law a bill to award the Congressional Gold Medal to the WASP as he lauded their "invaluable service to the nation."

"The Women Airforce Service Pilots courageously answered their country's call in a time of need while blazing a trail for the brave women who have given and continue to give so much in service to this nation since," President Obama said at the time. "Every American should be grateful for their service, and I am honored to sign this bill to finally give them some of the hard-earned recognition they deserve."

PART V

RELIGION AND CULTURE

15

A Cleric's Dream,
a Century in the Making

I ts towers have been called "boast-worthy," soaring higher than the towers of Westminster Abbey and Notre Dame. Its design, a priest who has long been leading tours of Cathedral Basilica of the Sacred Heart in Newark tells attendees, is "the most perfect…example of French gothic architecture in the Western Hemisphere." Its magnificence has wowed many a visitor, some of whom have seen Sacred Heart up close and many more who have only caught a glimpse of its majestic towers from afar. Yet most are unaware of the long and winding history of the cathedral, or of the nearly one hundred years that elapsed between its initial conception and its final dedication and when and how it became a basilica.

Indeed, Sacred Heart's story started in 1859. That's when the Most Reverend James Roosevelt Bayley, the first bishop of Newark, conceived of the idea of building a new cathedral in the city. Bayley, who had held that position since 1853, was not one to waste time. He found a plot of land on which to build the cathedral the very same year. That site, however—on the corner of High and Kinney Streets—was not deemed suitable. Neither was a second choice on South Park and Broad Streets.

The third time was the charm. The selected site, on a hilltop bounded by Park and Sixth Avenues, Clifton Avenue and Ridge Street, happened to be the highest point in Newark. It garnered the approval of one Jeremiah O'Rourke, both an architect and a trustee of Saint Patrick's Cathedral on Washington Street. Saint Patrick's cleric, Father George Hobart Doane, hailed the site as cathedral-worthy, noting that it commanded "a view of the Orange Mountains on the west and Newark Valley, the hills of Staten Island, and New York on the east." Bishop Bayley paid $60,000 for the plot and acquired a deed for the land in 1871.

A crucial step in the life of the future cathedral involved a trip overseas by O'Rourke, who would go on to be hired as Sacred Heart's architect, accompanied by Father Doane. The pair visited France, England and Germany in search of design ideas for what would become the official Diocesan Church of Newark. Initially, O'Rourke envisioned a rather small structure. But as the years went by, the scope expanded.

In 1872, before any work on the building had begun, Father Bayley was promoted and relocated to Baltimore. Several years later, his successor, Michael Augustine Corrigan, authorized the excavation of the site. But, as a booklet detailing the cathedral's history and heritage observes, "it was not until the arrival of Newark's third bishop, Winand Michael Wigger…that the project actually got off the ground."

Wigger, appointed in 1881, withstood relentless pleas from the city of Newark, which sought the land chosen for the cathedral to erect a new high school instead. But Wigger forged ahead. It was he who chose the name Sacred Heart, and in 1889, he formed a parish to serve the immediate area under that name. Construction of a small church and school soon followed.

Nothing more happened for a few more years, until, as the twentieth century approached, the project mushroomed in size and scope. In the late 1890s, major fundraising to cover the cost of the construction got underway and design proposals were solicited. The church formed an official Cathedral Committee and, in 1897, awarded a contract to architect O'Rourke. His plans called for an English-Irish Gothic cathedral, which he indicated would be a labor of love.

The official groundbreaking occurred in 1898, with Bishop Wigger digging the first shovelful. After that, work advanced so quickly that a date for laying the cornerstone was set. On June 11, 1899, more than one hundred thousand people gathered to witness the historic event.

Work continued at a rapid pace. By spring 1902, the history booklet notes, "the walls stood fifty feet at the nave," and work on the surrounding areas and the first four tiers of the towers was underway.

By then, however, the church leadership had changed once again. Wigger passed away in 1901. His successor, Bishop John J. O'Connor, urged O'Rourke to keep costs down, stressing the importance of not exceeding the $1 million estimate.

That, alas, was not to be. As the years flew by, costs rose exponentially. Miscalculations and conflict that arose between the architect and the general contractor early in the twentieth century were major contributing factors. By 1908, the church booklet states, the "feud had grown to such magnitude that work came to a grinding halt." Support—structural, not monetary—was the primary problem. As interior columns were erected, the contractor detected a shift in position. This was evidence, he maintained, that the supporting columns lacked the strength to withstand the weight of the stone that would rest on them.

The battle escalated, and two years later, O'Rourke was replaced. The new architect, Isaac E. Ditmars, ordered that all twenty-four pillars be removed—a major setback, albeit a crucial one. Excavations ultimately proved that the contractor was correct in finding that subsurface preparation had been insufficient. The end result was that the rock bed was leveled, the column foundations were redone and the original pillars were reset.

It is perhaps not surprising that besides making vital structural repair, a new architect would lead a shift in design as well. Instead of the English-Irish

Groundbreaking for Sacred Heart was in 1898; the dedication of the cathedral occurred in 1954. *Courtesy of Archdiocese of Newark.*

Gothic style originally planned, Ditmars favored a French Gothic cathedral. That, of course, required that new plans be drawn up. The Cathedral Committee accepted the new design in 1913, and work began anew.

Gone were the pointed spires, originally planned to be well over 300 feet tall. Ditmars questioned the ability of the foundations to support that height or the decorative features initially planned for the front towers. In their place would be two 232-foot-high towers—still surpassing those of Westminster Abbey and Notre Dame by a few feet and still tall enough to be visible for miles around.

Once again, work hummed along. By 1919, the cathedral had a slate roof and a copper flèche, the slender spire over the intersection of the nave and the transept of a Gothic church. Five years later, plate glass was installed in all the windows, "insulating the Cathedral from the weather."

Work on the interior led to other issues, including much debate about the type of limestone to be used. What's more, Bishop O'Connor had passed away in 1927, and the contractor was told to complete the crypt where he had been laid to rest. Today, the crypt contains the remains of five prelates.

That same year, Ditmars's contract was completed. Work ceased yet again for some years, and when the architect died in 1935, the cathedral was still unfinished. Enough had been done, however, that it was possible to celebrate Mass there. Thus, the first Mass at Sacred Heart Cathedral took place on May 1, 1928. It marked the installation of Bishop Thomas Joseph Walsh—the sixth chief prelate since the idea of building a new cathedral in Newark was born. Some four thousand worshippers filled the still-unfinished cathedral, which would be used on just nine occasions over the next twenty-plus years.

In 1950, at a celebration marking the fiftieth anniversary of his ordination, Walsh—who by then bore the title of archbishop—announced a major push to complete the cathedral. Fundraising once again took center stage, as the cost had gone from its initial $1 million price tag to a final tally of $18 million.

Sadly, Archbishop Walsh did not live to see Sacred Heart's completion. He passed away in 1952. His successor, Archbishop Thomas Aloysius Boland, was appointed the following year, and on October 19, 1954, he dedicated the "mighty Cathedral." It had taken ninety-five years, two architects and the leadership of seven prelates to bring the masterpiece to fruition.

Sacred Heart is the fifth-largest cathedral in North America. It covers more than forty-five thousand square feet and is equal in size to Westminster Abbey. It is both longer and taller than New York City's Saint Patrick's Cathedral and has a main rose window that is second in size only to the

An aerial view of the majestic Cathedral Basilica of the Sacred Heart. *Courtesy of Archdiocese of Newark.*

one at New York's Saint John the Divine. Indeed, Sacred Heart has three rose windows that have been described as "a trifecta of glass masterpieces." Art historians consider the splendor of Sacred Heart's stained glass to be surpassed only by that of Chartres Cathedral in northern France, the priest who serves as its historian and docent has said.

The design incorporates materials, including wood, stone and marble, from a variety of countries. The stained-glass windows hail from Munich, Germany, and are reported to be among the world's finest. Tower bells were cast in Padua, Italy, and tested by bell experts at the Vatican. Woodwork and pews were crafted from Appalachian oak and walls from New England granite and limestone from Indiana. Bronze doors from Rome adorn the cathedral, which has an altar made of Italian marble from a quarry in Pietrasanta.

Behind the main altar and surrounding the sanctuary are a series of small chapels representing the ethnic and racial diversity of the Archdiocese of Newark at the time the cathedral was being built: St. Patrick (British Isles),

St. Lucy Filippini (Italian, Portuguese), St. Boniface (German), St. Stanislaus (Polish, Slovak and Hungarian) and St. Anne (Hispanic, African and Asian).

The Lady Chapel, directly behind the main altar, is particularly impressive. Dedicated to Our Lady of Grace, it has an altar crafted from Carrara marble and three chandeliers made of hand-cut crystal. Unlike the small chapels, the Lady Chapel is a space where Mass can be served.

October 4, 1995—forty-one years after Sacred Heart's dedication— marked another critical date for the cathedral. On that day, Pope John Paul II visited Sacred Heart, accompanied by President Bill Clinton and First Lady Hillary Clinton. After serving Mass, the pope conferred upon it the designation of basilica, thereby changing its official name to Cathedral Basilica of the Sacred Heart. The cathedral is one of 91 "minor" basilicas in the United States and some 1,800 worldwide. There are only four "major" basilicas in existence, all in the Diocese of Rome.

Visitors who look to the left of Sacred Heart's main altar will spot the symbols that signify this notable designation. There is a red-and-gold-striped *ombrellino* (umbrella), its traditional papal colors representing the relationship between the basilica and the pope. The ombrellino sits atop a coat of arms representing the Archdiocese of Newark, the Sacred Heart of Jesus and the coat of arms of Saint John Paul II. A gold bell post, or *tintinnabulum*, and a set of crossed keys—the keys of Saint Peter—symbolize papal authority.

Today, visitors come from far and wide, not only to worship but also to tour and experience the splendor of the Cathedral Basilica of the Sacred Heart. Guided tours are conducted on the first Sunday of the month following Mass at noon. Individuals are allowed in during the week by appointment. Group tours can be arranged on weekdays as well.

The cathedral also hosts a concert series, giving visitors an additional opportunity to take in its beauty. Besides showcasing world-class musicians, many of the concerts feature the Cathedral Basilica's "awe-inspiring organ." This magnificent pipe organ—the largest among Catholic churches in the Western Hemisphere—has 9,513 pipes. NJ Advance Media's Mark Di Ionno famously described them as "ranging in height from the size of a pinkie fingernail to a 37-foot pipe that sounds like a ship's horn." The organ, it has been said, produces "some of the purest melodies in the world," sounds that are far too good to be missed.

16

TIBETAN ART AT THE ALTAR

The fourteenth reincarnation of the Buddha of Compassion—known throughout the world as the Dalai Lama and to Tibetans as Yeshin Norbu or Kundun—was born in 1935. And although he remained unaware of it for the next several decades, His Holiness has had a lifelong bond with New Jersey's largest city—or, more precisely, with its flagship museum. Almost from its inception, the Newark Museum of Art was a major collector of Tibetan art and artifacts. More importantly, the museum installed a Tibetan Buddhist altar, believed to be the first in the nation, in the year of the Dalai Lama's birth.

The start of what would become one of the world's most extensive collections of Tibetan treasures can be traced to 1910, just a year after the Newark Museum was founded. It all began with a chance encounter between a founding trustee and an American physician as they traveled by ocean liner from China to the United States.

As the two men struck up a conversation, Dr. Albert Shelton (a medical missionary) told Edward Crane (the trustee) that he had spent years working in eastern Tibet. Shelton went on to say that he had an extensive collection of the country's art and artifacts stored in the hold of the ship. Among the hundreds of objects he was carrying home were sculptures, masks, headdresses, jewelry, manuscripts, sacred paintings, ritual instruments and more.

As a missionary, Shelton had cared for people from every walk of life, from nomads to nobility. While some of the treasures he brought home with him had been gifts from patients, many more were recovered from monasteries and temples that were destroyed during the lengthy border wars between China and Tibet. The collection was hailed in *Newark Arts* as "amazingly diverse…comprising some of the finest items ever to have left Tibet."

In addition to Shelton's desire to preserve the valuable art and artifacts, he was carting them home to America in hopes of raising money to support his mission. Crane had another idea. Newark Museum, he asserted, which at the time was housed on the top floor of the Newark Public Library on Washington Street, was an ideal venue for an exhibit of Tibetan treasures. After some persuasion, Shelton acquiesced.

The exhibition that resulted, held in 1911, generated so much excitement that the museum trustees wanted more. They commissioned Shelton to seek more treasures on subsequent missionary trips to Tibet. An article in the *Christian Science Monitor* refers to a letter in which Shelton lamented the difficulties of sending such art and artifacts from Tibet to the United States. In an outline of the shipping charges, the article states, Shelton enumerated the cost of going 460 miles from Batang to Tachienlu by yak ($2.00); 1,000 miles by steamer to Shanghai ($0.75); and Shanghai to New York ($3.50). The total cost, the article states, was $9.75!

After the doctor died in 1922, the museum was able to find (and ship) additional Tibetan treasures, purchasing several missionary collections from northeastern Tibet. As the museum amassed one of the finest Tibetan art collections in the world, its trustees gained an understanding and appreciation of the importance of the sacred objects. Thus, the idea of building a Tibetan Buddhist altar was born.

Originally conceived of as a temporary installation that would provide a meaningful setting for these ritual objects, the altar was erected and painted by artists working with the Works Progress Administration, part of the federal New Deal program started during the Great Depression that successfully put millions of Americans to work. Although still a notable achievement, it lacked the rich colors and intricate yet proscribed patterns that traditional Buddhist altars are bedecked with. That, of course, is no surprise, since none of the artists had ever seen an authentic Tibetan altar. They had nothing more than black-and-white photographs to go by and no Tibetans on hand to guide them.

The finished product was impressive if not colorful. Indeed, the altar proved to be so popular that it remained on display for more than fifty years, from 1935 until the late 1980s, when plans for an expansion of the museum, including an extension of the entire Asian display and a new, more authentic-looking Tibetan altar, began to take shape. In the interim, it attracted Tibetan dignitaries and His Holiness, the Dalai Lama.

No group of Tibetans is believed to have stood before the altar until 1948, when a trade delegation from Tibet visited the museum. And, despite the Dalai Lama's auspicious connection to the altar vis-à-vis the date of his birth, His Holiness did not see it until 1979. He made the first of four visits to the museum that year; a second followed in 1981. On both occasions, he was delighted not only by the altar but also by the richness and variety of the museum's Tibetan exhibit.

Before work on a new altar could begin, the original altar needed to be deconsecrated and dismantled. While it had never been officially consecrated, museum curators and staff had come to understand that the many visits and practices of Tibetan monks, dignitaries and other Buddhists had in fact resulted in the sanctification of the sacred space. So in January 1988, the Venerable Ganden Tripa Rinpoche performed the deconsecration ceremony for the local Tibetan community.

The spiritual leader began by formally recognizing the Buddhas believed to reside within the altar and asking them to temporarily return to their celestial home, or "Pure Space." He then addressed the many sacred images, paintings, manuscripts and ritual objects that were part of the altar. Before these religious artifacts were packed up and put away, the Ganden Tripa asked them to remain in storage until they could be incorporated into the altar that would soon be built.

The current altar, unlike the first, was designed and painted by a Tibetan man with expertise in sacred art. Phuntsok Dorje, who served as the Newark Museum's artist-in-residence in 1989 and 1990, mastered his craft at a Tibetan monastery. He began his studies there when he was only nine years old. A team of Tibetan consultants and scholars worked with Dorje on the design and execution of the intricate patterns on the altar and on the script of sacred scrolls.

A consecration ceremony on September 23, 1990, marked the final step. It was led by the Dalai Lama, with the assistance of ritual masters, lamas and attendants. His Holiness began by making three prostrations and presenting a white *kata*, a silk scarf that symbolizes primordial purity. Lighting a flame in a golden butter lamp came next, followed by prayerful chanting.

The chants included the mantra of interdependent origination—a prayer that set the stage for the rest of the ceremony by evoking universal Buddhist truths. Prayers were invoked to arouse compassion for all sentient beings, make the universal mandala offering and take refuge in the Buddhas.

The Newark Museum of Art's authentic Tibetan Buddhist altar was consecrated by the Dalai Lama in 1990. *Diane Gail.*

Next came the tossing of grains, carried out between chants, as a means of ensuring that the prayers were "solid" and "true." The dorje and the bell, emblems of tantric Buddhism evoking power and wisdom, were held in special positions.

Finally, the Dalai Lama issued an invocation to the Buddhas, calling on them to enter the altar and remain there. The invocation, repeated three times, is intended to remind the Buddhas of their vow to teach enlightenment to all who seek it. With that vow comes a promise not to enter into final nirvana until this task has been completed. Ultimately, the museum brochure notes, "the structural sections of the 1935 altar were sealed in a recess of the new altar, in accordance with the Tibetan tradition of linking the spiritual presence of the old with the new."

This altar is a dazzling sight, particularly notable to all who remember what the museum's original altar looked like. Colors sparkle like jewels: electric blue, vivid crimson and emerald green, adorned with sunshine yellow and gold pigment. Drawings and symbols that have appeared on Tibetan Buddhist altars for well over one thousand years are visible, the lotus, garlands, curtains of color and a wheel of Buddhist doctrine among them. The creation evokes a Pure Land not unlike the one in the celestial home that the Buddhas who vacated the old altar were asked to return to, thus ensuring that the new altar serves as a suitable abode for the Buddhist deities.

At the center of the altar sits a gilt copper image of the historical Buddha Shakyamuni. A museum brochure highlights its importance "as the focus of devotion." The image is enhanced by a small throne, with the Buddha sitting cross-legged, soles of the feet visible, on a lotus seat and perched in a traditional lotus pose. The Buddha's right hand forms a gesture of "earth-touching," or witnessing; his left hand rests on his lap in a meditative pose. The Buddha's face is tranquil, his eyes partly closed and mouth gently smiling. Long earlobes convey renunciation of the world while also reminding visitors that Shakyamuni was born to royalty and thus wore heavy earrings that caused the deformity.

On one side of the Buddha is a statue of the deity of compassion—an eleven-headed, eight-armed figure that some have compared to a Christian saint. On the other side is a stupa, or reliquary, that represents Buddha's death (parinirvana). Sometimes compared to a Christian cross, the stupa is symbolic of the Buddha's attainment of nirvana. It is also thought to symbolize the five elements: earth, water, fire, air and ether.

Behind the opening of the altar are a set of tankas, or painted scrolls, depicting the principal of the five Buddha families. Each represents one form of awareness. And in front of the Buddha are offerings—rice, flowers and incense among them—often placed there by practitioners to express their devotion to the principle of enlightenment.

Nine years after the altar's consecration, Phuntsok Dorje returned to the museum to paint the entry to the altar. His visit coincided with the reinstallation of "From the Sacred Realm: Treasures of Tibetan Art in the Collection of the Newark Museum." And the Dalai Lama—winner of the 1989 Nobel Peace Prize—returned to the museum for the fourth time in 2011, when he came to Newark to participate in a three-day peace summit. The historic event brought together scores of distinguished speakers from around the world, joining with the Dalai Lama to further the cause of nonviolent conflict resolution.

17

JUST JAZZ

"Discover Jazz…Anywhere, Anytime, on Any Device."

That's the tag line on the website of WBGO, 88.3 FM.

While many people know of the station's existence, few are aware of its history or of how it went from having virtually no listeners to becoming the self-proclaimed "global leader in jazz radio, broadcasting from the jazz capital of the world."

Although that description of the city might be a bit of a stretch, Newark has long been a key player in the jazz scene. In *The Encyclopedia of Newark Jazz: A Century of Great Music*, author Barbara J. Kukla wrote that Newark became known as "Swing City," "a major hub on the jazz map of the world."

Newark and jazz have long gone hand in hand. One part of the reason, Kukla wrote, was the purity of the city's water in the early part of the twentieth century. That, in turn, led to Newark being known for its breweries. At one time, the nation's "Big Five" brewers—Ballantine, Hensler, Krueger, Feigenspan and Weidenmeyer—were all located in the city, along with other notables like Schaefer, Pabst and Anheuser-Busch. Because Newark was also a manufacturing hub, there was an enormous opportunity to sell beer to workers at day's end. Thus, large numbers of bars opened up. "By 1938," according to Kukla, "Newark had more than 1,000 saloons, one for every 429 residents." On a per capita basis, that was more than any other American city.

And what better way to lure people into a tavern than to feature a piano player, a singer or a combo? Newark had its share of home-grown major jazz artists, the Divine Sarah Vaughan, James Moody, Wayne Shorter and

Viola Wells (aka Miss Rhapsody) among them. Then, too, because of the city's proximity to New York City, the big swing bands, led by notables like Duke Ellington, Count Basie and Lionel Hampton, would play in Newark's larger venues on their way in and out of Manhattan.

Opportunities abounded, too, because of the sheer number of clubs. *The Encyclopedia of Newark Jazz* includes extensive lists, not only of musicians and singers but also of swing-era bands and jazz venues in the city. The latter, an A-to-Z list of two hundred places where musicians played live in Newark, begins with the Adam's Theater and ends with Zig's. Not surprisingly, the city was seen by some as the ideal setting for jazz radio.

Today, WBGO reaches some three hundred thousand listeners in the metropolitan area each week. But its scope has long extended far beyond that. Through programs like *Jazz Night in America*, produced in partnership with National Public Radio and Jazz at Lincoln Center; its long-running Kids' Jazz Concert Series; and home-grown shows that have aired on national public radio stations, its reach has extended to millions more nationwide. The station was the first in the country to focus on just jazz, all the time. It began broadcasting in 1979 and adopted a 24/7 format in 1980, when New York–based WRVR Jazz Radio did an abrupt switch to country-and-western music.

WBGO was an early adopter of streaming technology, says marketing manager Brandy Wood, making it possible to reach jazz enthusiasts worldwide. "We have listeners on every continent (Yes, we have a member in Antarctica!)," she observes. WBGO.org boasts that members from Malaysia, Turkey, Germany, Japan, Israel, Italy, Mexico, Brazil and Great Britain echo the sentiment of a listener from South Africa who sent an email declaring the station to be "so inspiring."

All told, the station is supported by more than seventeen thousand members, plus grants and contributions from corporations, foundations and government organizations. Deliberately established as an independent station licensed by Newark Public Radio, WBGO Jazz was New Jersey's first public radio station.

It is important to note, however, that the station existed long before its call letters became synonymous with jazz. WBGO dates to 1948, when the Newark Board of Education acquired the license and began broadcasting from the fourth floor of Central High School. For years, the station covered school events like spelling bees and football games, as well as serving as a teaching tool for students interested in broadcasting. But because it was reserved for school-related events, no broadcasting occurred when school was not in session. That, and the fact that the signal at 88.3 FM had the capacity to reach "upwards of 20 million listeners," led observers to conclude that the pre-jazz radio station was "chronically underutilized."

That was the status quo in the 1970s, when the station came to the attention of Robert G. Ottenhoff, then a communications specialist at the Office of Newark Studies. A division of Rutgers University, the office was dedicated to helping the city find positive ways to rebuild community and reenergize residents in the aftermath of the infamous 1967 rebellion.

At the time, those who started WBGO jazz radio recall, Newark was a bit of a media desert. The *Newark Evening News*, one of two major city papers, had shut down in 1972; WNET, the public television station, had relocated to New York City; and there were no radio stations other than the one licensed by the Newark Board of Education. Activists wanted a homegrown news outlet and started to think that a new iteration of WBGO could fit the bill. Questions abounded about the possibility of transferring its license and how the station might best be used.

That's where jazz came in. Ottenhoff, generally thought of as the "new" WBGO's founder, was an avid jazz fan, and Newark was a jazz city, so he proposed that genre as the focus. "We wanted a format that reflected the diversity of the area," he recalled, "and no format does that better than jazz." (In a strange bit of irony—some call it fate—Ottenhoff, who goes by Bob and whose middle name is George, bears the same initials as the station's call letters.)

Seizing an opportunity to realize this vision, Ottenhoff and others lobbied the board of education to transfer the broadcasting license to New Jersey Public Radio. In 1977, the board agreed, and WBGO Jazz went live two years later. In the early years, however, there were an ample number of observers who predicted doom and gloom.

In a 2021 New Jersey PBS special, *The WBGO Story: Bright Moments from Newark to the World*, individuals involved in the start-up vividly recall the sentiments of those who were sure the venture would fail. Some insisted it was foolhardy to start a radio station in Newark only a decade after the race riots. Others were convinced that an all-jazz format would never catch on, noting that no radio station had ever tried it and that it would be impossible to attract an adequate number of supporters. Conversely, others feared that if the station did survive, its founders would waste little time moving it out of Newark, just as WNET TV had done.

Naysayers aside, a review of the circumstances in which the jazz station got its start reveals legitimate cause for concern. In the early days, the station had no money, no listeners, barely any relationship with musicians and a scant supply of records. Nor did WBGO have its own headquarters. At first, the newly licensed, independent, not-for-profit station continued to operate out of the fourth floor of Central High.

What WBGO did have in abundance was dedication, confidence and the "unbridled enthusiasm" of Bob Ottenhoff. Steve Robinson, an experienced radio executive who joined the station early on, urged Ottenhoff to hire Dorthaan Kirk, who would later become known as "Newark's First Lady of Jazz."

The widow of Rahsaan Roland Kirk—a renowned multi-instrumentalist hailed as "one of the great modern jazz artists of the twentieth century" who passed away in 1977—Dorthaan Kirk knew little about the business of broadcasting. But she had intimate knowledge of the music world. Traveling the world with Rahsaan while he performed had given her the opportunity to forge strong bonds with a multitude of jazz greats. These relationships proved invaluable to WBGO's success.

"She was our ambassador to the music world," Ottenhoff recalled on the PBS special. "She would call and say, 'We're a brand new station, you haven't heard of it yet but would you come over and do an interview?' And they came." She "probably dealt with every jazz luminary who performed in the '70s and the '80s and the '90s," he added. "It's a Who's Who of the music world."

Notably, too, Kirk was the driving force behind many of the creative projects WBGO undertook. In addition to the widely acclaimed children's concert series, she introduced jazz vespers at Bethany Baptist Church and launched the Dorthaan's Place Jazz Brunch series at New Jersey Performing Arts Center (NJPAC), among other programs. In 2020, Kirk was the recipient of the A.B. Spellman NEA Jazz Masters Fellowship for Jazz Advocacy, considered the highest honor in the jazz world.

NJPAC is less than a minute from 54 Park Place, WBGO's headquarters since its early days. Not long after the jazz station began operating, the people running it found what was then a vacant building directly across from Military Park in the heart of downtown. Ottenhoff approached the owner with what must have sounded like a preposterous proposition: "We don't have any money, but we want to buy the building." And that is exactly what happened. The sale went through, and the station moved in. But in the early years, the space used for broadcasting wasn't a lot better than the one they had left.

With no money to renovate, the action occurred on the second floor—a crowded, uncomfortable space that lacked air-conditioning—and got

WBGO headquarters at 54 Park Place, a street recently renamed Wayne Shorter Way. *Wikipedia.*

extremely hot. It wasn't unusual in the early days, commentators on the PBS special recalled, to walk in and find announcers clad only in their underwear.

Soundproofing was a serious problem as well, so anytime the station was airing live, fans could not be used. The flush of a toilet would echo on the air as well, so the bathroom was off-limits during interviews and pledge drives. On one occasion, when someone forgot and the sound reverberated during a fundraising event, Steve Robinson is said to have quipped, "And here's someone from Flushing."

In the early days of WBGO Jazz, announcers began asking listeners to call. And that's just what they did. It wasn't long before this tiny, nonprofit entity had attracted a virtual army of volunteers, including many listeners who were willing to pay to hear music they could have accessed for free. A high point for the station occurred when the team discovered that the average pledge to WBGO surpassed that of WQRX, New York Public Radio's classical music station

In June 2023, WBGO—now in its forty-fourth year—launched its latest fundraising event. Titled 4400 Members in 72 Hours Summer Fund Drive, the drive's aim was to ensure WBGO's continued success by turning 4,400 listeners into new members. That's 100 for every year!

PART VI
NEWARK NOW

18

Urban Farming Grows Up

For many years and to many people, urban farming was an oxymoron. Add Newark to the equation, and the concept was even harder to imagine. Who would've thought that a farm in New Jersey's largest city could succeed in growing kale that's "sweeter," arugula that's "perfectly peppery" or watercress that's "zesty"—or that many more equally flavorful varieties of Newark-grown greens would not only survive but thrive as well?

Newark's unlikely farming prowess begins to make sense as more information about the process emerges. First comes the revelation that the greens owe neither their taste nor any other characteristic to the dirt in which they're planted or the sunlight in which they're bathed. There's a simple reason for that: The produce in question is not grown in soil. Nor is it exposed to the sun. Kale, arugula, bok choy, red-leaf lettuce and more grow indoors in Newark, their roots exposed to air and misted with a "growing cloth" patented by AeroFarms, a leader in sustainable "ag tech" farming.

Edward Harwood, an inventor, entrepreneur and researcher long affiliated with Cornell University's College of Agriculture and Life Sciences, was the chief scientist at AeroFarms until his death in 2021. He was also the pioneer of its successful technique. Harwood spent years in pursuit of a way to successfully grow crops with minimal resources. One of the biggest challenges was finding a cloth that would work as a growing medium and soil substitute.

As part of his lengthy research, Harwood visited a leading fabric store again and again, testing virtually every kind of cloth imaginable. When

The greens produced at AeroFarms are grown aeroponically, without soil, sun or pesticides. *Courtesy of AeroFarms.*

none had the desired effect, he invented his own: a thin white fleece that holds the seeds as they germinate and keeps them upright as they grow. Known to those at AeroFarms as a "misting cloth," Harwood's invention is made from recycled plastic water bottles, and it is patented. The misting cloths are recyclable themselves. They can be completely cleaned to avoid cross-contamination, thus enabling them to be reused again and again.

Built on the grounds of an old steel mill in Newark's Ironbound section and opened in 2015, the AeroFarms facility once laid claim to the title of the world's largest indoor vertical farm. That distinction, however, had but a seven-year tenure. In 2022, AeroFarms outdid the record it had set, opening a new indoor farm in Danville, Virginia, with twice the growing space.

AeroFarms began to take shape in the early 2000s, when Harwood and its cofounders, CEO David Rosenberg and marketing director Marc Oshima, were based in Upstate New York. Not surprisingly, "Why Newark?" is a question Rosenberg and Oshima have grown accustomed to hearing. Or, as the headline of a recent New Jersey Advance Media article put it, "What's this farm doing in the middle of Newark?"

As it turns out, there are multiple reasons.

For starters, both Oshima and Rosenberg had ties to the city and its surrounding suburbs, Rosenberg through a previous business and Oshima vis-à-vis family members. Indeed, several years before opening the Ironbound facility, Harwood set up a mini-farm—the prototype of the aeroponic system that AeroFarms uses—at Philips Academy, a charter school in Newark.

Newark has other features that attracted the founders of AeroFarms. For one thing, it has long been a transportation hub, with easy access to New York and in proximity to rail, air and shipping ports. AeroFarms's Ironbound facility is also within a short distance of a major distribution center for ShopRite, a primary outlet for the farm's produce. What's more, Newark is a rapidly developing tech hub. This is especially crucial because, as the company notes on its website, "At its heart, AeroFarms is technology driven," striving to sustainably feed Newarkers, Americans and, ultimately, everyone on the planet.

The opportunity to make a difference was a key part of the decision to base AeroFarms's headquarters in Newark. As the New Jersey Advance Media headline concluded in answer to its own question as to what the firm was doing here, AeroFarms was "trying to change the world."

In the Newark area, Oshima said, AeroFarms was working to eliminate a food desert, selling greens to residents directly and poised to open mini model indoor farms like the one at Philips Academy at two additional Newark schools. Students love eating greens from the salad bar that they're helping to grow.

In 2023, however, the company announced a major shift: the transition of its commercial food production to the new facility in Virginia. Newark will remain AeroFarms's global headquarters and center for research and development, however. With more than one hundred thousand square feet of space for R&D, AeroFarms said in a press release, the focus here will be on the advancement of "next-generation crops and indoor vertical farming solutions." The company also has a state-of-the-art research center in Abu Dhabi.

AeroFarms's leaders and others in the ag tech industry assert that R&D is increasingly critical. In the last thirty years, the world has lost some 30 percent of its arable land, the combined result of overdevelopment, population sprawl and climate change. Hence the importance of growing produce indoors and vertically, which requires minimal space. Aeroponic farming, advocates say, is the most effective means of growing crops with limited resources. While it is akin to and often labeled hydroponic farming, in fact there are differences. The main point to keep in mind is that aeroponic farming is more reliant on air (aero), hydroponic farming on water (hydro).

Mathias Levarek, CEO of Agronomy, a corporate leader in vertical farming, puts it this way: "Oxygen is the key for nutrient delivery at the root level." In regular hydroponics, he adds, "the roots are immersed in a substrate and covered with water, whereas in aeroponics, the roots are hanging in the air and always have 100 percent availability of oxygen."

Thus, while hydroponic farming cuts way back on the amount of water needed to grow crops, aeroponic farming decreases it even further. AeroFarms boasts that its crops use up to 95 percent less water than traditional farming. Pesticides are eliminated entirely, and fertilizer use is kept to a minimum.

Space, like water, is an increasingly scarce commodity, and aeroponic farming pays high dividends here as well. AeroFarms claims to use less than 1 percent of the land required by conventional farming to produce the same volume of crops. Put another way, its yield per square foot is a whopping 390 times that of traditional farming. Its indoor farms have extremely high ceilings—the Newark facility accommodates twelve layers of stacked "grow tables" in rows that are eighty feet long and thirty-six feet high. LED lights function much as natural sunlight would.

All of this makes it possible for rapid growth. The typical gestation period for greens produced by AeroFarms is a scant two weeks, yielding as many as twenty-six harvests per year. The flavor, AeroFarms' marketers contend, is enhanced as well—hence its use of descriptors like "sweeter," "more peppery" and "zestier."

In an article in an organic farming journal, an expert in regenerative agriculture compares the uptake of nutrients by greens grown hydroponically versus aeroponically. The latter, the analysis suggests, results in less nutrient waste and yields higher amounts of nitrogen, phosphorus, potassium, calcium and magnesium.

Regardless of the precise methodology, the future would seem to be bright for indoor vertical farming, a result, it appears, of a critical combination of innovation and necessity. While AeroFarms was one of the early adopters of ag tech, such operations, each using somewhat different means and methodology, are cropping up not only across the United States but also in nations worldwide. Bowery, a large vertical farming company headquartered in New York City, has "smart farms" in multiple states, where, the company asserts, hundreds of crops can be grown indoors with a minimum of space and scant use of ever-more-scarce resources.

AeroFarms' greens and herbs are marketed at major outlets, including ShopRite, Stop & Shop, Walmart, Whole Foods and more. It also produces hops—flowers, also known as seed cones, of the hop plant *Humulus lupulus*, used in making beer—for a major brewery, and it markets various types of produce to many Fortune 100 companies. In 2021, AeroFarms and the World Economic Forum entered into a deal with Jersey City, the state's second-largest city. The first municipal vertical farming program in the country, the partnership committed to building ten vertical farms in public places in Jersey City, such as senior centers, schools, public housing and municipal buildings. The aim of the program is to produce some nineteen thousand pounds of vegetables each year and make them available to city residents at no charge.

Fruits are on the horizon as well. In 2021, AeroFarms entered a multi-year R&D partnership with Hortifrut S.A., a Chilean corporation that is a leader in berry production. The two ag tech leaders will jointly research and develop blueberry and caneberry production in vertical indoor farms. (Caneberries are varieties of berry that grow on hard, woody stems known as canes and include raspberries, blackberries and boysenberries.) In announcing the deal, AeroFarms's CEO, David Rosenberg, harkened back to New Jersey's distinction as the home of the cultivated blueberry. This was, he noted, the state in which, in 1910, "blueberries were domesticated for the first time."

Vertical farming is likely to go beyond greens and berries. In a recent article, "Vertical Farming—No Longer a Futuristic Concept," scientists at the Department of Agriculture's Agricultural Research Service reported investigating the growth not only of small berries but also of "fruiting vegetables" such as tomatoes and peppers and on larger fruit-tree crops such as apples, citrus fruit and peaches. The researchers noted, too, that in a quest for facilities in which vertical farming can be established, they had begun repurposing shipping containers and old abandoned warehouses. "Converting them into vertical farming environments not only breathes life back into discarded infrastructure but also puts fresh produce in parking lots and urban centers," they said. Vertical farms, they concluded, are cropping up all over—"in deserts, high-population urban areas and other places that traditional open-field farming is not practical."

19

FROM INJUSTICE TO HEALING

I n the spring of 2020, days after the world reacted with horror to the murder of George Floyd at the hands of the Minneapolis police, Newark staged a protest. In light of reports of sporadic violence at Floyd protests in some cities and the still-vivid memory of Newark's fifty-three-year-old rebellion and the decades of setbacks that city residents endured in the aftermath, individuals with an affinity for New Jersey's largest city held their collective breath. *Please don't let anything happen to derail Newark from its hard-won journey of revitalization and resilience.*

They need not have worried. On May 30, some twelve thousand people converged on City Hall to march peacefully. Reporters noted that on the rare occasion that someone in the crowd appeared ready to shatter the peace, Newarkers reacted swiftly and forcefully: "Get out of our city," protesters shouted at a man who appeared poised to shatter a storefront window. "You're not from here," someone added. "You're not gonna mess things up for us."

So successful was the afternoon rally that a commentator tweeted, "The world needs to know what happened in Newark today." Amid the city's lingering reputation for trouble, which flew in the face of the on-the-ground reality, it might have been more apt to focus on what did *not* happen that day. No looting or serious property damage occurred. No one was seriously injured. No tear gas, rubber bullets or guns were fired, and no one was arrested.

Instead, thousands protested peacefully. The marchers carried banners and placards. They chanted. They yelled. They danced, and they sang. "Down, down, do your dance, do your dance," the words of the "Cupid Shuffle" rang out, as scores of protesters and an occasional police officer shuffled in tune.

A bronze statue of George Floyd, sitting on a park bench outside of Newark City Hall. *Helen Lippman.*

The rally was organized by the People's Organization for Progress. Larry Hamm, chair and cofounder, addressed the crowd and led the march with Mayor Ras Baraka by his side. Baraka spoke, too. He told the protestors that he shared their outrage and noted that his late father, the renowned activist and poet Amiri Baraka, had been beaten during the 1967 uprising.

The police had a positive presence as well. Newark's public safety director had advised the police to stand down, overlook minor offenses on the day of the rally and avoid engaging angrily with the protestors. Their primary job on the day of the rally was simply to direct traffic and keep the flow.

The most fraught moments came early in the evening. With no more than a couple hundred protesters remaining, a small but rowdy group made its way to the city's First Precinct on Seventeenth Avenue—the very place that was the flashpoint for the 1967 uprising. On a sweltering midsummer day in July of that year, Newarkers living in substandard public housing nearby watched in horror as white policemen dragged a Black taxi driver out of his car and beat him so long and so hard that a (false) rumor that he'd been killed rapidly spread. The next morning, an enraged protestor slammed a crowbar through a window of the precinct (known as the Fourth Precinct at the time), and the riots were off and running. The melee went on for five days—days and nights filled with Molotov cocktails, fires, shootings and looting. It later emerged that the very officers whose job it was to quell the violence, including the National Guard and New Jersey State Troopers, fired more than 12,000 shots.

All told, more than 700 people were injured, 1,500 arrested and 26 killed, with most of the deaths caused by rifles fired by law enforcement. Property damage was massive as well, amounting to some $115 million in today's dollars. Other aspects of the rebellion's legacy are harder to quantify, but in the words of one prominent Newarker, "It left us dead for decades."

On this site on July 12, 1967, there began a civil disturbance that took the lives of twenty-six people and forever changed our city.

May this plaque serve as a symbol of our shared humanity and our commitment to seek justice and equality.

Dedicated July 12, 2007 by the Citizens of Newark

1967   CITY OF NEWARK INCORPORATED 1836   2007

A. Booker and the Newark Municipal Council

The precinct where the1967 rebellion began—marked with a commemorative plaque—now houses the Office of Violence Prevention and Trauma Recovery. *Helen Lippman.*

Twenty-first-century Newark is far different, and on the evening of May 30, 2020, a much more hopeful story played out. With police officers lined up outside of the historic precinct in the aftermath of the Floyd march, there were provocations that could have led to confrontation. One man climbed atop a police vehicle and shook a fist; someone else threatened to slash tires. But in a tribute to the city's years-long focus on nonviolence and police training in de-escalation, calmness reigned. With nothing notable happening, the crowd soon dispersed, and the remaining stragglers drifted away.

Less than a month later, the old precinct, still in use albeit with its first-floor windows boarded up, was back in the news. On June 25, 2020, Mayor Baraka stood in front of it to announce the city's newest, and likely most sweeping, anti-violence measure to date. "This is a historic moment," the mayor said, proudly proclaiming that the Newark City Council had passed an ordinance creating a permanent Office of Violence Prevention and Trauma Recovery the previous day.

To fund the office, popularly known as OVP, 5 percent of Newark's public safety budget—about $12 million annually—was set aside. Its mission is to prevent violence and help those affected by it—whether as victims or perpetrators—confront, cope with and overcome the devastating effects.

In highlighting plans for the OVP, Baraka emphasized not only how it would function but also the way in which it came into being. "Other cities have created these types of offices as 'policy,'" the mayor said, "but we have made it a law." That is a crucial difference, he stressed, because while elections occur and decision-makers and policies change, it takes far more to change a law.

The OVP operates citywide, with interventions occurring where they're needed, but it is headquartered at the Seventeenth Street Precinct. "There is a powerful symbolism about reclaiming a territory and remaking it in service of those persecuted, collectively transforming its use and meaning," a recent report on public safety in Newark observed. Like the city itself, the historic building, with all the painful memories of racial injustice it represents, is slated for transformation. Plans call for it to be incorporated into a new facility on the site, envisioned as a combined healing center and civil rights museum.

Architectural plans for the Newark Community Museum of Social Justice—conceived of as a place for learning and storytelling as well as trauma recovery—emerged as a result of a design studio led by Roger Smith, a principal at the global architecture firm Gensler and a professor at New Jersey Institute of Technology's (NJIT) Hillier School of Architecture and Design. Before working to reach consensus on a design proposal, Smith's students were charged with researching both the conditions leading up to the '67 rebellion and the economic, cultural and social climate in Newark today.

Renderings of the design, unveiled at a press conference in July 2021, show "the vestigial brick structure wrapped in three floors of cantilevered steel mesh boxes," as described in an NJIT press release. The idea is for much of the old space to be converted into galleries and offices for the OVP, while the new structure would feature a café, meeting rooms and a community center. The design includes an outdoor plaza that would replace a dilapidated vacant lot, featuring ample seating, abundant greenery and banks of trees to represent the lives lost during the 1967 riots.

"The new design embraces the original building in a dialogue about a traumatic past and a more hopeful future," Smith told those gathered. "It preserves the collective memory of the community through exhibitions highlighting Newark's history of activism against racial injustice. It's also a place for healing, where people can learn conflict resolution and violence prevention," he said.

The work of the OVP has been ongoing, starting well before the building itself began to take shape. Soon after the office was established, director Lakeesha Eure had a team of social workers and outreach staff in place. The goal, she noted, was to have one social worker for every ten police officers.

And the OVP rapidly began amassing a string of successes. One is the Safe Summer Initiative. The program focuses on identifying young community members at risk of being involved in violence in any way and stepping in before the devastation occurs to engage those at risk in supportive programs and educational activities instead. Another is a grants program. In March 2022, the mayor announced eight community-based recipients of grants as part of a $1 million violence-reduction initiative under the OVP. Recipients include programs that work to foster positive interaction between Newark youth and its police officers, help young people with mental health issues and create opportunities for individuals ages sixteen to twenty-four who are out of school and unemployed. The selection of the organizations, Eure said, demonstrates "a strategic commitment by Mayor Baraka and the City administration to ensure the availability of community-based violence prevention resources across all five wards." A similar call for grant recipients went out the following year.

Newark now has a place for those who have been harmed by past episodes of racial injustice and violence to address the trauma, a place where they can remember and talk about the events and hopefully continue on their journey, Eure said. But just as important as remembering and healing from past incidents, those involved in the vision of the OVP agree, is to make the center a place that the city's youth can embrace. That became especially evident, Roger Smith said, in listening to the thoughts and concerns of those in his design studio. The students rejected the notion of a staid civil rights museum, he observed, envisioning a place with vibrant, high-tech, interactive exhibits instead.

Then Smith switched gears again, harkening back to a planned feature of the new facility that older residents—at least those old enough to recall the city's pre-'67 days—would remember and embrace. "We are restoring The Milk Bar!," he announced, referring to a beloved burger and shake joint that was destroyed in a fire in 1967. The crowd erupted in cheers.

The museum, Mayor Baraka stated in a recent strategic planning report, will be inaugurated "to honor the history of the fight for racial and social integration in our city." At press time in the fall of 2023, construction of both the museum and the Milk Bar had not yet begun.

20

MURAL CITY

As murals go, Newark is a relative newcomer. Philadelphia, which some tout as the mural capital of the world, launched its public-art initiative more than four decades ago. In contrast, Newark did not issue a call to muralists until well into the twenty-first century.

Nonetheless, the city's abundance of public artwork is rapidly growing. At last count, there were well over one hundred murals within city limits. Most, but not all, are outdoors. One of the most recent additions, a 350-foot mural titled *Between the Future Past* by an Ecuadorian-born Newarker known for his large-scale artwork, is a notable exception.

Seen in the arrival hall and concourse level of Newark Liberty International Airport's new Terminal A, the mural draws on the indigenous heritage and native Kichwa language of its creator, Layqa Nuna Yawar. It also features people of various colors and ethnicities and from all walks of life, including a young Lenni Lenape boy, Newark's own world-famous jazz singer Sarah Vaughan and the photographer Dorothea Lange, as well as everyday laborers. Flora and fauna fill out the mural, with images of everything from bog turtles to egrets, roses, violets and the New York skyline.

People passing through the airport, visitors to Newark and longtime residents alike may experience the city's ever-growing mural collection as an unabashed surprise and, often, an unexpected delight. Nonetheless, readers would be justified in wondering why murals, which by their very nature are public, are featured in a book about Newark's *hidden* history.

The answer is twofold. For one thing, the proliferation of murals in Newark is new enough that many people have no idea they exist. As a recent article in an arts journal put it: "When you come to Newark, you cannot miss graffiti tags, stenciled airbrush messages on buildings and tattered flyers plastered on poles. However, you can miss some dope art tucked in corners or back streets." This essay, coupled with the steps the city is taking to publicize its ever-widening collection of public art, may help to draw attention to works that are often eye-catching and always thought-provoking.

Then, too, Newark murals deserve a place in this book for another important reason. The city holds a notable, but not widely known, record in the national mural milieu. It is home to what is unquestionably the longest mural on the East Coast and quite possibly the longest in the country. Titled {*Portraits*}, it runs for 1.39 miles along McCarter Highway (Route 21), approximately the length of twenty-five football fields. Indeed, one observer, Caressa Losier, who studies street art and focuses on it on her blog, *trending-in.com*, describes {*Portraits*} as "one of the longest mural sites in the world."

Completed in 2016, {*Portraits*} was the collective effort of eighteen artists who worked by night for two intense weeks. Aided by stadium lights, projectors and several assistants, the muralists used some 1,500 gallons of paint to memorialize their visions. {*Portraits*} marked the inauguration of the Gateways to Newark project, dedicated to using public art and landscape improvements to beautify entryways into the city. *The Future Nurtures the Past*, a large mural that runs along Raymond Boulevard from University Avenue to Lock Street, serves a similar purpose.

Murals began popping up in Newark more than a dozen years ago, when the city planning office enlisted the support of local arts organizations. In 2014, when Mayor Ras Baraka, a poet, artist, educator and former city councilman, took office, he embraced the beautification project and kicked it up a notch. The Neighborhood Mural Revitalization Program began that year. Today, old and new buildings alike, time-worn retaining walls, battered fences and any number of other large surfaces have been repurposed as canvases—for inspiring messages, uplifting images and themes of strength and resilience designed to boost the spirit and offer hope.

At first, the murals, like other evidence of Newark's burgeoning revitalization, were clustered in and around downtown. As the positive changes began to extend into other neighborhoods, public art did, too—a point blogger Losier emphasizes on her blog.

"Unlike neighboring art capitals," Losier writes, in Newark, "there's no limit to which side of town you might stumble upon a mural proudly

The 1.39-mile {*Portraits*} mural was the work of eighteen artists. *Helen Lippman.*

depicting the city's diverse Black population. Black Americans, Nigerians, Haitians, Jamaicans, Guyanese and so many other Black cultures have helped shape the variety of faces, shapes and subjects found in the city's large-scale murals." Among those featured on her blog are *Black Butterfly and Love*, an image of a pig-tailed young Black girl supported by glorious butterfly wings, on Clinton Avenue; *Three Doctors* on Sixteenth Avenue, based on the true story of three boys who grew up fatherless and poor and went on to become physicians; and *The Reflective Black Body*, also by Layqa Nana Yawar, on Jeliff Avenue. That mural, which shows two seemingly separate faces gazing intently at each other, was inspired by the author Ta-Nehisi Coates, who wrote in his memoir, *Between the World and Me*, that "how one should live within a black body, within a country lost in the Dream, is the question of my life."

Some of the elements of {*Portraits*}, which covers a stretch of roadway that an estimated one million vehicles drive along each month, address similar issues. Based on the belief that it is important for city residents to see images of people who look like them, one muralist incorporated portraits of young people living in a nearby housing project into his portion of the wall.

All told, {*Portraits*} consists of sixteen panels, each with a distinct color palette and artistic interpretation of the single theme that unites them: Newark history and culture. Together, they cover the weary, century-old Amtrak retention wall that runs along (and below) the railroad for which the neighborhood just east of it, the Ironbound, is named.

One of the {*Portraits*} panels portrays the mundane. Awash in primary colors, images reveal people engaged in everyday activities, like walking, talking, eating and commuting. Another features iconography reflective of both the city and the state: a lion's head, like the one that holds pride of place at nearby Newark Penn Station; a body of water reminiscent of Port Newark; and a fish that calls to mind a New Jersey brook trout. Yet another, mindful of the symbolism of a railway, designed blocks that resemble the quilts in which enslaved women embedded coded messages to guide fugitives headed north on the Underground Railroad.

In June 2020, in the shadow of the murder of George Floyd at the hands of the Minneapolis police on May 25, Newark launched its Social Justice Public Art Initiative. Seven murals with that as the theme were completed within that year alone.

Among the first to be dedicated was *Will You Be My Monument*, inspired by the city's removal of a long-standing Christopher Columbus statue in a downtown public space. Previously known as Washington Park, it has since been renamed Harriet Tubman Square. A colossal monument to the famed abolitionist, large enough for visitors to walk around and into, to read and hear stories about Tubman's life and work and to get close enough to touch her chiseled face, now stands in its place.

Will You Be My Monument is the collaborative work of a writer, a photographer and a designer. Its focal point is an image of a child, an eight-year-old girl whose picture was taken as she celebrated her birthday at the park. The design of the mural, which is the height of a four-story building, is meant to emphasize that while Black girls are important and powerful, they often remain invisible, the photographer, Scheherazade Tillet, said. *Will You Be My Monument*, Tillet observed, invites "us all to see ourselves through the gaze of Black girlhood."

Not long after *Will You Be My Monument* made its appearance came another multistory mural celebrating the fight for social justice. The unveiling of *Sojourner Truth, Founding Mother* was timed to coincide with the one-hundredth anniversary of the passage of the Nineteenth Amendment, which granted women the right to vote. The towering portrait highlights the noted African American activist, suffragist and abolitionist. Sojourner Truth's message,

Mayor Baraka said at the dedication of the mural honoring her, "remains as current and important now as it did then."

Rise Up Fallen Fighters, a mural in which the late poet and playwright Ntozake Shange serves as a focal point to represent Black resilience and liberty, echoes the social justice theme. It depicts Shange surrounded by figurative symbols of unused models for the Statue of Liberty.

In 2021, at the Newark Arts Festival in July, the city's interactive public-arts map made its premiere. So, too, did a dramatic new mural on a building that is ten stories high. Called *Magnitude and Bond*, it is the work of a Black women's artist collective. The towering mural celebrates Gladys Barker Grauer and Breya Knight, both described as "esteemed figures in the rich history of arts and poetry in Newark."

The work celebrates two additional Black poets. The mural's title comes from a quote by noted poet Gwendolyn Brooks. And a sprawling banner draped across the mural carries the immortal words of the prominent Black poet Lucille Clifton: "Come celebrate with me that every day something has tried to kill me and has failed."

In December 2021, Baraka heralded the completion of *The Future Nurtures the Past* on Raymond Boulevard, another linear "gateway" mural. This one is double-sided, stretching along both sides of the roadway between Lock Street and University Avenue for nearly half a mile. Completion took two months, as it involved landscaping and repair work as well as creating the artistic vision of a pair of muralists. Andre Leon and Robert Ramone, both of whom grew up in north Newark, went on to forge a collaborative public-art practice called Rorshach. Although the pair are no strangers to oversized public works of art, this was their largest project to date. It took five hundred gallons of paint to complete the work.

On each side of Raymond Boulevard, the ground-up mural features whooshes of color and free-flowing forms, metaphorically held together by oversized human hands. The artists chose to honor women, including those who cared for and nurtured them as well as others they deemed worthy of honor—a student, a single mother and a survivor of abuse among them. In keeping with the name of the mural, Rorshach incorporated graffiti that had been posted on the walls years and sometimes decades earlier. The artists recreated multiple layers of writing and markings to honor and preserve messages left by Newarkers in years past. At the dedication of *The Future Nurtures the Past*, Mayor Baraka stated, "The public murals seen around the city tell our stories, inspire, and empower our community." This one, he added, beautifies "a major and historic artery in our downtown."

The Whitney Houston mural is made of one thousand pounds of hand-cut glass in a rainbow of color. *Diane Gail.*

Music has served as an inspiration for other murals, particularly those associated with and supported by Newark's Grammy Museum Experience. A mural on Central Avenue depicts Haitian American rapper Wyclef Jean hovering over a sweeping piano keyboard. A newer and more dramatic Grammy Museum–commissioned mural is a vivid, twenty-eight-foot mosaic of Whitney Houston. Made of one thousand pounds of multicolored glass, her image sparkles on a pink background on the side of an apartment building on William Street.

Want to learn more? Use the interactive Public Art Map at https://newarkarts.org/publicartmap.

21

A PLACE TO CALL HOME

ewark has a population of nearly three hundred thousand, including more than one thousand city dwellers who have nowhere to live. Among the city's homeless—known to those who work to support them as residents without addresses—are a couple of hundred who are particularly shelter averse, put off by the lack of privacy, loss of freedom and perceived safety risk associated with city shelters.

In late 2020 and early 2021, as winter weather worsened and COVID-19 cases soared, the problems associated with homelessness intensified. Individuals living on Newark streets, often in dilapidated tents or battered cardboard boxes, faced a heightened risk from the pandemic. Overcrowded shelters made the spread of the virus more likely, and the importance of giving visitors additional space of their own exacerbated a chronic shortage of beds.

March 2021 marked a turning point.

"Many of our residents without addresses have been traumatized by the system that was created to serve them," Mayor Ras Baraka said on March 8 as he proudly announced the opening of Newark Hope Village. Located on Newark Avenue on the corner of Central Avenue on a lot that had long sat vacant, Hope Village was touted as a "no requirements-come-as-you-are" safe haven. "It is a low-barrier residency," said Craig Mainor, executive director of United Community Corporation (UCC), the agency charged with overseeing the management of Hope Village. "As long as you are not a danger to yourself or others or the community, you are welcome here."

Hope Village comprises seven shipping containers, each divided into four separate units that can house either a single adult or a couple. All told, there are twenty-eight units, each with a windowed door with lock and key. Inside each unit are bunk beds, storage space, a heater and a small dresser. All have heating and air-conditioning and fully comply with federal, state and city residency codes. Each container has bathrooms and private showers and a multipurpose area, complete with refrigerator and microwave. Brightly colored tables and chairs adorn the outside of the containers, which were tastefully decorated by a group of local artists.

Building Hope Village—which involved retrofitting standard steel shipping containers based on an architect's design—cost about $900,000, paid for with money from the federal CARES Act, as well as some city and state funds. But the units can be used over and over and are easily adaptable to the needs of subsequent residents. In the end, the designer, Steve Schneider of the California-based nonprofit Homes 4 the Homeless, told the *Star-Ledger* days after Hope Village's opening, that the cost is "roughly $10,000 per bed."

Residents receive multiple services, including treatment for substance abuse and behavioral health care, case management, assistance with family reunification, job search and help in finding permanent housing, as well as re-education in life skills. Mobile units deliver breakfast and lunch, Mainor

The exterior of Hope Village is adorned with brightly colored doors and picnic tables. *Courtesy of United Community Corporation.*

added, noting that residents often refrigerate leftovers from lunch and save them for dinner. After a short time, a need for mobile washers and dryers also became apparent. Until laundry facilities were brought in on a regular basis, Mainor reported, residents often rinsed out clothing in the bathroom sink or shower, then tracked sopping-wet items back to their personal quarters. Not only did this do a poor job of cleaning the clothes, but the constant dripping also damaged the flooring in the units.

In the years since the idea of using containers for housing was introduced, the concept has proven successful. Nonetheless, observers often question the wisdom of putting people in boxes. But, as Schneider emphasized in the *Star-Ledger* interview, no one is "just taking a container off a boat and putting people in it." By the time the containers are retrofitted and made fully compliant, he said, the entire feel of the structure has changed.

Among the benefits, in addition to the low cost, are the security and durability of the steel shipping containers, their accessibility (via Port Newark) and the speed with which they can be adapted. "We turned this around," Mainor boasted, "from the first meeting with the architects to handing the keys to the residents, in 90 days." While Newark was not the first municipality to seize on the idea, it was the first to go from concept to reality on an emergency basis within such a tight time frame.

One often overlooked benefit of container living is the very fact that residents of Hope Village have an address: 79 Newark Avenue, plus their unit number. Not only is that important when filling out job applications, but it also enables individuals to receive Social Security checks and other payments due them. What's more, residents can come and go as they please without worrying that their belongings will be stolen or rifled through.

Initially, city planners expected Hope Village to be a three-month buildout followed by a three-month placement. At the end of ninety days, they imagined, individuals would be ready to move on, ideally into more permanent housing. That, Mainor acknowledged, proved to be quite a learning experience. "We realized it was unfair to have a time limit," he said more than a year after the village opened. While some residents were ready to move on in a relatively short time, a lot more were not. In May 2022, Mainor observed, "many of our guests have been here for more than a year, and there is no plan to remove anyone. Where would they go?"

Despite the often longer-than-expected stays, people living in Hope Village continue to progress. In the spring of 2023, Mainor happily reported that several longer-term residents had recently transitioned to more permanent housing. Overall, the container village had proven to be so successful that a second one was in the works. "We've broken ground and are working on the next phase of the building—the placement of utility lines"—at Hope Village II, Mainor said in April. "We're hoping people will be moved in by the end of June."

Located on Elizabeth Avenue, Hope Village II has twelve units and twenty-four beds. Reflecting the realization that people often take longer than originally anticipated to move on to more permanent housing, these units are larger. Each can house two people and has a common living space, a kitchenette and two bedrooms. "It's like a two-bedroom apartment," Mainor said.

Duration of stay, of course, was not the only "teachable moment" that the first Hope Village presented. Another was the importance of identifying ways of more carefully screening potential residents. Mainor recalled a couple who had been living in a tent at Penn Station. Soon after offering them a unit in the Newark Avenue container village, he said, "we realized this was an unhealthy relationship because of domestic violence." In addition to better screening methods, the program administrators realized, "we needed to communicate the importance of self-preservation."

For individuals who turned out to be well suited to the program, however, living in Hope Village often brought unanticipated benefits. Citing the case of one young woman with persistent mental health challenges, Mainor noted, having a safe place to call home was an immeasurable boost to her recovery. Not only was she now able to make and keep appointments with providers that the chaos of homelessness had often led her to miss, she also had a safe place in which to store her medication—a virtual impossibility for anyone living on the street.

Another lesson—an eye-opener, Mainor reported—was the importance of detecting unspoken, often hidden barriers that prevented some individuals from taking advantage of help that was offered. He recalled a man who had inexplicably turned down multiple opportunities to move into his own apartment, until the program administrators discovered that he was anxious about being on his own and fearful of being unable to handle the expenses associated with independent living. With that awareness, UCC was able to provide not only rental assistance but supportive guidance as well.

With residents of Hope Village I continuing to thrive and Hope Village II on the verge of opening, Craig Mainor is deeply thankful. "Our agency does a lot in the city," he said. "We have a lot of programs designed to help those who need us most." And, while they're all important, "this particular project is the one I am so so proud of. To see people who were literally sleeping on concrete streets move into their own places? I get goosebumps. I'm just in awe."

BIBLIOGRAPHY

Atkinson, Joseph. *The History of Newark, NJ: Narrative of its Rise and Progress.* Newark, NJ: William B. Guild, 1878.

Beer Can Collectors of America. *United States Beer Cans: The Standard Reference of Flat Tops and Cone Tops.* Fenton, MO: BCCA, 2001.

Branch Brook Park Alliance. Cultural Landscape Report, Treatment, and Management Plan for Branch Brook Park, Newark, New Jersey. Vol. 2: *History of the Park and Critical Periods of Development,* 2002. https://branchbrookpark.org.

Cathedral Basilica of Sacred Heart. *History and Heritage, Roman Catholic Archdiocese of Newark.* www.newarkbasilica.org.

Cummings, Charles. "Knowing Newark: Trinity Cathedral Marks 250 Years of Religious, Historical Contributions." *Star-Ledger,* May 2, 1996. https://knowingnewark.npl.org.

———. "Knowing Newark: Yes, General George Washington Slept Here. Often, in Fact." *Star-Ledger,* May 16, 1966. https://knowingnewark.npl.org.

Despommier, Dickson. *The Vertical Farm: Feeding the World in the 21st Century.* London: Picador, 2010.

Dietz, Ulysses Grant. *The Glitter & the Gold: Fashioning America's Jewelry.* Newark, NJ: Newark Museum, 1997.

Di Ionno, Mark. "Newark's 'Old First Church' Going Strong at 35." *NJ Advance Media,* December 15, 2016. https://www.nj.com/news.

———. "Sacred Heart Cathedral—Newark's Stairway to Heaven." *NJ Advance Media/NJ.com,* April 16, 2009. https://www.nj.com.

Dismore, David. "Today in Feminist History: Suffragists Kick Off a Protest Hike from Newark to the Nation's Capital." *MS Magazine*, February 12, 2019. https://msmagazine.com.

Geisheimer, Glenn. "Newark Religion. Trinity Episcopal Church." *Old Newark*. http://newarkreligion.com.

Grover, Warren. *Nazis in Newark*. Piscataway, NJ: Transaction Publishers, 2003.

———. "The Newark Communist Party: 1919 to the New Deal." *Newark History Society*, December 3, 2012.

Howlett, Charles, and Audrey Cohan. *Loyalty Oaths and Academic Witch Hunts*. Rockville Centre, NY: Faculty Works: Education, 2008.

Kelsey, Frederick Wallace. *The First County Park System: A Complete History of the Inception and Development of the Essex County Parks of New Jersey*. Charleston, SC: BiblioLife, 1905.

Kindy, David. "Why the P-47 Thunderbolt, a World War II Beast of the Airways, Ruled the Skies." *Smithsonian Magazine*, November 24, 2020. https://www.smithsonianmag.com.

Kukla, Barbara. *The Encyclopedia of Newark Jazz: A Century of Great Music*. West Orange, NJ: Swing City Press, 2017.

McManus, Fran. "The Return of Newark Cider." *Edible Jersey*. September 1, 2015. https://ediblejersey.ediblecommunities.com.

Moore, Kate. *The Radium Girls: The Dark Story of America's Shining Women*. Naperville, IL: Sourcebooks, 2017.

New Jersey Suffrage Timeline. *Votes for Women!* Trenton: New Jersey State Library, updated May 18, 2023. https://libguides.njstatelib.org.

Nielsen, Audrey. "A Public Safety 'Ecosystem': Newark's Success Story." *The Crime Report*, June 15, 2022. https://thecrimereport.org.

Parker, Allison. "Mary Church Terrell: Black Suffragist and Civil Rights Activist." National Park Service, December 14, 2020. https://www.nps.gov.

Rae-Turner, Jean, and Richard Koles. *Newark, New Jersey*. Charleston, SC: Arcadia, 2001.

Roberts, Rebecca Boggs. *Suffragists in Washington, D.C. The 1912 Parade and the Fight for the Vote*. Charleston, SC: The History Press, 2017.

Schrecker, Ellen. *The Age of McCarthyism: A Brief History with Documents*. 2nd ed. Boston: Bedford/St. Martin's, 1994.

Schultz, David. *House Un-American Activities Committee. The First Amendment Encyclopedia*. Washington, D.C.: CQ Press, 2009. https://www.mtsu.edu.

Stamberg, Susan. "Female WWII Pilots: The Original Fly Girls." *NPR.org*, March 9, 2010.

Stearns, Jonathan. *First Church in Newark: Historical discourses, relating to the First Presbyterian church in Newark; originally delivered to the congregation of that church during the month of January, 1851*. https://rutgers.primo.exlibrisgroup.com.

Su, Hannah. "Newark Artist Collaboration Honors Its Home City with 13 New Murals." *Architect's Newspaper*, June 8, 2022. https://www.archpaper.com.

Tuttle, Brad. *How Newark Became Newark: The Rise, Fall, and Rebirth of an American City*. New Brunswick, NJ: Rutgers University Press, 2009.

U.S. Committee on Un-American Activities. *Investigation of Communist Activities in the Newark, N.J., Area*. Vol. 1. London: Forgotten Books, 1955.

Wees, Beth Carver. *Nineteenth-Century American Silver. Heilbrunn Timeline of Art History*. New York: Metropolitan Museum, 2004. www.metmuseum.org.

Wolff, Theodore. "This Majestic Newark Cathedral Is Sacred and Superlative." *New Jersey Monthly*, July 1, 1981. https://njmonthly.com.

ABOUT THE AUTHOR

Helen Lippman was born and raised in Newark. She earned a BA in English from Rutgers-Newark and an MA in journalism from New York University. After covering health care and medicine for many years, she began writing articles and giving talks about her hometown. Her book *To Newark with Love: A City, a Family, a Life* was published in 2023.

Lippman's work has appeared in a variety of publications, including GoNomad.com, *Hadassah Magazine*, *New Jersey Monthly*, the *New York Times* and *Wanderlust*. She lives in Montclair, New Jersey, with a cat named Barry.